CORONATION

The Men & Machines of the Royal Air Force Coronation Review at Odiham
15 July 1953

Eric Bucklow

First published in Great Britain in 1998 by
Hikoki Publications
16 Newport Road, Aldershot, Hants, GU12 4PB
Tel: 01252 319935 Fax: 01252 655593
E.mail hikoki@dircon.co.uk
© 1998 Hikoki Publications

All rights reserved. Apart from any fair dealing for the purpose of private study, research, criticism or review, as permitted under the Copyright, Design and Patents Act 1988, no part of this publication may be reproduced, stored in a retrieval system, or transmitted in any form or by any means, electronic, electrical, chemical, mechanical, optical, photocopying, recording or otherwise, without prior written permission. All enquiries should be directed to the publisher.

ISBN 0 951899 6 0

Edited by Barry Ketley
Artwork by David Howley
Cover artwork by Mark Rolfe
Design by Hikoki Publications
Printed in Great Britain by
Hillmans, Frome, Somerset

Distribution & Marketing by
Midland Publishing Ltd
24 The Hollow, Earl Shilton, Leicester LE9 7NA
Tel: 01455 233 747 Fax: 01455 233 737

Caption to front cover: *Gloster Meteor F.8, WK722/A of 601 Squadron wearing the tail stripes indicating the CO's aircraft. Finish is the overall silver sported by most of the day fighters of the period, but which was rapidly being replaced by camouflage once more on the newer types as the Cold War got into its stride*

Captions to rear cover:
106 Gloster Meteor F.8, WH374/A of 63 Sqn. Inset: 63 Sqn. badge.
107 Gloster Meteor F.8, WH378/N of 54 Sqn. Inset: 54 Sqn. badge.
108 Gloster Meteor FR.9, WH542/B-K of 2 Sqn. Camouflaged. Inset: 2 Sqn. nacelle marking.
109 Gloster Meteor NF.11, WD649/C of 264 Sqn. Inset: 264 Sqn. badge.
110 Canadair Sabre F.4, XB673/G of Sabre Conversion Flight, Wildenrath, Germany. Inset: Provisional badge of the S.C.F.).
111 Canadair Sabre 2, 19151, BT-151 of 441 Sqn. RCAF. Inset: 441 Sqn. badge.

1 Caption to title page: *A detailed look at the nose armament and starboard Griffon engines of Avro Shackleton MR.2, WL747, of 269 Squadron. Finish is the classic maritime grey and white with the Coastal Command badge just visible on the nose. Boeing Washington B.1, WF565, of 207 Squadron towers in the background*

ALSO AVAILABLE

Forever Farnborough
Flying the Limits 1904-1996
by
Peter J. Cooper AMRAeS
ISBN 0 951899 3 6

Royal Naval Air Service 1912-1918
by
Brad King
ISBN 0 9519899 5 2

Luftwaffe Emblems 1939-1945
by
Barry Ketley & Mark Rolfe
ISBN 0 9519899 7 9

Aufklärer
Luftwaffe Reconnaissance Units & their Aircraft
by
David Wadman, John Bradley & Barry Ketley
ISBN 0 9519899 8 7

Luftwaffe Fledglings 1935-1945
Luftwaffe Training Units & their Aircraft
by
Barry Ketley & Mark Rolfe
ISBN 0 9519899 2 8

FORTHCOMING

The Secret Years
Flight Testing at Boscombe Down 1939-1945
by
Tim Mason
ISBN 0 951899 9 5

Eyes for the Phoenix
Allied Photo-reconnaissance Operations
in South-east Asia in World War 2
by
Geoff Thomas
ISBN 0 951899 4 4

Stormbird
Flying through fire as a Luftwaffe ground-attack
pilot and Me 262 ace
by
Oberst (i. R.) Hermann Buchner
ISBN 1 902109 00 7

Courage Alone
The Italian Air Force 1940-1943
by
Chris Dunning
ISBN 1 902109 02 5

FROM TIGER TO SWIFT
Rehearsals for a Queen

The subject of this book is Her Majesty's Coronation Review of the Royal Air Force, which was held at RAF Odiham on 15th July 1953. Unlike the earlier Coronation flypast on 2nd June which was affected by bad weather, the Review flypast of 641 aircraft took place in good conditions and was supported by a large static display of 318 aircraft along with displays and parades covering all aspects of the Royal Air Force.

A number of articles have appeared in magazines over the years but coverage of the individual aircraft involved in the flypast has been scanty. The main aim of this booklet is to identify as many of the participating aircraft as possible. The static display list is an amalgamation of five independent enthusiasts' lists (the public were allowed access to the aircraft after the official part of the Review was over). For the flypast, details of pilots who took part are listed in a document held in the Officers' Mess at RAF Bentley Priory, although it does contain a few inaccuracies and omissions which have been corrected where possible. Unfortunately, the document does not include details of other crew members. In the few cases where this information has been included in the text, details have come mainly from letters received. Decorations have not been included as full details are not available. Aircraft identities have been taken from two main sources, namely pilots' log books and Squadron Form 541s (Bomber and Coastal Commands only).

Pilot log-books often identify an aircraft from its code letter only, so an appendix has been included which lists some of the units involved, showing the aircraft which were on strength as at 15th July 1953. This information has been taken from the aircraft record cards held at the Royal Air Force Museum and, where known, the aircraft code letter is also shown. All the other aircraft in the formation lists have also been checked against the record cards to ensure that they belonged to the units concerned apart from those mentioned in the notes. The photographs have come from several sources and as many as possible were taken on the 15th July, although a few depict rehearsals for the event. If anyone can fill in any of the gaps, particularly by tracing those pilots who have not so far been located, or by providing serial-to-code tie-ups, please contact the author via the publisher.

I am indebted to all the participating aircrew and their next-of-kin who have written to me with information

2 Above: Meteor NF.11s of 29 Squadron, based at Tangmere but operating from West Malling, low over the Berkshire countryside during a flypast rehearsal. Nearest is WD603, 'C', being flown by F/Ls L.R. Schofield and Davis. Further back is WD600, 'S', with F/L J.M. Hocking and F/O Sheppard. Leading the pack is S/L E.B. Sismore in WD722, 'E'. All are finished in the standard nightfighter camouflage scheme of the period of Dark Green and Medium Sea Grey. Just visible in the foreground is the wing of the camera ship flown by Sgt E.I.V. Lee, outside man of the formation

about the aircraft and their recollections of the event. Thanks must also go to the aviation enthusiasts who have helped me with information and photographs, particularly Geoff Cruikshank, the late John Rawlings, Ray Sturtivant, Roger Lindsay, Frank Hudson, Alan Wright, John Eagle, Peter Cooper, Mike Bowyer, Bruce Robertson, Peter Green, Dick Ward and Cyril Peckham. I would also like to thank the following people and organisations for their assistance: Staff of the Personnel Management Centre of the MoD at Gloucester (for their help in forwarding letters); Elaine Jones of the Quadrant Picture Library; Graham Day of the Air Historical Branch, MoD; Ken Hunter at the RAF Museum (for letting me delve into the individual aircraft record cards); Wing Commander Dauncey of the RAF Benevolent Fund; Wing Commander Martin of the RAF Association; Wing Commander R. Peacock-Edwards; Flight Lieutenant Ken Delve; Danny Boon of The Aircrew Association; Flying Officer Sara Barclay of the Central Flying School; David Jenkins of the Joint School of Photography, RAF Cosford (who provided the excellent vertical photo of the static display) and BAe via Mike Stroud. Crown Copyright material in the Public Records Office is reproduced by kind per-mission of the Controller of Her Majesty's Stationery Office. Last, but not least, to members of the British Aviation Research Group who did the initial work towards publication, and to the publisher, Barry Ketley, and illustrator, David Howley, who brought the book to life.

Preparations and the great day

This Review was to be only the second Royal Review of the Royal Air Force in its 35 year history (the first one had commemorated the Silver Jubilee of King George V, taking place at Mildenhall and Duxford on 6th July 1935). Preparations for the flypast started approximately one month before the Review with wing leaders flying their routes to the 'gate' at Leavesden then on to Odiham before dispersing. During this period, the various units relocated to the airfields from which they were to operate for the Review itself.

The route and required timing over Odiham (30 seconds between formations, except for Bomber and Coastal Command aircraft which were to use 45 seconds) was a highly complex plan, not only for the inbound run, but also for the dispersal back to base. Since most of the navigation was conducted using stopwatch and map, it says a lot for those involved that times over Odiham during the later rehearsals and on the 15th July were generally within 5 seconds of target. Extra navigation aids provided at the 'gate' (327° magnetic, 2,400 yards from Leavesden airfield) were a EUREKA beacon and an MF beacon. There was a line of ground marker flares along the $33^{3}/_{8}$ miles from the 'gate' to Odiham, while at Odiham itself there were three Cathode Ray Direction Finding consoles, each operating on a different frequency.

Many of the letters from participating pilots mention incidents during rehearsals, such as Wing Commander Wallace leading 48 Meteors into a particularly dense-looking cloud with the comment "What a nuisance chaps; steady as she goes, don't bump into anyone"! There were several cases of civilian (and occasionally RAF) aircraft straying into the path of the formations, usually without much time for avoiding action from either party. Because of the tight timing tolerance, some of the early rehearsals resulted in one formation sliding over the top of another. Since these incidents usually occurred when the cloud-base was low (as governed by the law more politely attributed to Murphy), the clearance between the lower aircraft and the ground was sometimes marginal. It is perhaps surprising, considering the difficulties involved, that there was only one disaster during the rehearsals, when on 8 July two Meteors of 257 Sqdn flown by F/L A.H. Blewitt and P/O R. Forrest collided. Both pilots were unfortunately killed.

As slower aircraft flew past first, followed by formations at ever-increasing speeds, there were several close calls between formations making their way back to base until more specific departure routes were worked out. The AOC of 11 Group remarked in his report that there was "some difficulty" in getting test pilots to do sufficient practices, and that the pilot of the Victor turned up for several of the rehearsals in a Canberra. Considering the uncertain serviceability of prototypes during a development programme, it possibly was not their fault. Personal experience suggests the following conversation: Pilot: "When is the wonderplane going to be ready? I have to take-off at 12.43 for the practice". Engineer: "Tuesday".

Turning to the day of the Review itself, 15th July 1953 turned out to be a typical summer's day with only small amounts of cloud in the morning, but with cumulus developing during the afternoon so that by the time of the flypast conditions were quite bumpy. The morning was taken up by a parade representing the home-based Commands, the Royal Air Force Regiment, the Womens Royal Air Force, Apprentices and Boy Entrants as well as the massed bands of the RAF and WRAF. The parade was inspected by the HRH The Queen and the Duke of Edinburgh, after which a march-past took place. The Royal party then left for a lunch in the Officers' Mess as four Venoms using smoke inscribed 'ER' in flowing letters at about 10,000 feet.

Over lunchtime the spectators were treated to a 'warm-up' for the flypast, consisting of various aircraft going about their normal tasks. This started with a CCF Corporal in a Tiger Moth from Fairoaks on his first solo cross-country flight, a Hastings returning from a flight over the North Pole, a Canberra which had flown to Malta and back that morning and another Hastings bringing in 32 casualties from Korea.

The Royal party then returned to tour slowly along the lines of 318 parked aircraft, stopping at intervals to talk to representatives of various Commands and Units. When Her Majesty asked the CO of 664 AOP Squadron if his aircraft were present, he pointed them out in one of the rear ranks. She remarked sympathetically "So they put them behind". As this part of the review ended the four CFE Venoms returned to sky-write 'ER', in block capitals this time.

The main event started at 3.39·50pm with a Sycamore trailing the RAF Ensign flying past at 75 knots. It was followed by Training and Transport Command aircraft, Sunderlands, Lincolns (144 knots), Washingtons, Coastal Command aircraft and Hastings (169 knots). The jets came next, including Australian and Canadian Squadrons, starting with Vampires at 265 knots and progressing through Venoms and Meteors (300 knots) to Canberras, Sabres and Swifts. The last machines to fly over were single examples of the 'V-bomber' and swept-wing fighter prototypes, ending with a Swift F.4 travelling at 580 knots noisily displaying its reheat.

This parade of 197 piston-engined aircraft and 444 jets took 27 minutes to pass and was rounded off by the Venoms which returned to sky-write 'VIVAT'. As *The Times* correspondent wrote, "to fly formations of aircraft in such a Review as the RAF Coronation flypast is to share some of the feelings of the second row in a dancing troupe. It is fairly certain that individual performances will be noticed only for their faults. What matters is the total effect". As one of the spectators, the author thought that the total effect was very impressive indeed. The day was well rounded-off when the barriers were removed and the public were allowed to inspect the ranks of immaculately turned-out static display aircraft. During this, the last official flypast of the day was made by a Mosquito PR.34, RG194 of 58 Squadron, on a photo-run.

3: The first Royal Review of the RAF, June 1935. King George V, accompanied by his sons (later King Edward VIII and King George VI) alighting from his Rolls-Royce at the beginning of a tour of inspection of the Handley Page Heyford bombers of 99 Squadron, then based at Mildenhall

4: 15 July 1953. The Royal party during the tour of inspection after lunch, but before the Review Flypast. The open tourer Rolls-Royce appears to be one of those used for the same purpose in 1935! The vantage point is from the rear rank of the left flank, just to the left of the crescent, behind the Canberras of Bomber Command

5 Left: Light bombers 1. Here are the Hawker Harts of 57 Squadron, seen during the Royal Review of June 1935 at Mildenhall. Note the squadron number on the wheel chocks

6 Below left: Light bombers 2. De Havilland FB.9 Vampires of 19 and 48 MU, 15 July 1953

7 Below: A view of the rear rank of the left flank shortly before 15 July as there are no crowds and there has been a recent shower of rain. Nearest are the Canberras of 10 and 57 Squadrons. Behind are Varsity T.1s of various schools, with the tails of the dark blue Neptunes of 203 Squadron just visible. In total 57 aircraft can be seen

8 Right: Odiham on 15 July complete with crowds. The dark triangle at the top of the picture is the tailplane of the camera ship, (a Varsity) possibly F/O Twigger's aircraft

THE STATIC DISPLAY
From air and ground

The aircraft are listed in their parking order (left to right, facing the crowd), except for the first and second ranks of the Crescent where they are listed in serial order.

LEFT FLANK		
1st (front) rank:		
19163/BT-163	Sabre 2	441 Sqdn
19151/BT-151	Sabre 2	441 Sqdn
19142/BT-142	Sabre 2	441 Sqdn
19158/BT-158	Sabre 2	441 Sqdn
19159/AM-159	Sabre 2	410 Sqdn
19176/AM-176	Sabre 2	410 Sqdn
19144/AM-144	Sabre 2	410 Sqdn
19141/AM-141	Sabre 2	410 Sqdn
19152/52	Sabre 2	439 Sqdn
19155/55	Sabre 2	439 Sqdn
19188/88	Sabre 2	439 Sqdn
19195/95	Sabre 2	439 Sqdn
WH238	Meteor T.7	78 Wing
WH220	Meteor T.7	78 Wing
WX981	Meteor FR.9	20 MU
WX976	Meteor FR.9	20 MU
WX978	Meteor FR.9	20 MU
WX975	Meteor FR.9	20 MU
WE913	Meteor F.8	23 Sqdn
WK658/G	Meteor F.8	63 Sqdn
WK754/WH-S	Meteor F.8	APS
VZ530	Meteor F.8	AFDS

WK943/N	Meteor F.8	257 Sqdn
WK972/H	Meteor F.8	CGS
WL259	Meteor FR.9	12 MU
WH549	Meteor FR.9	12 MU
WH554	Meteor FR.9	12 MU
WH550	Meteor FR.9	12 MU
WG950/X-65	Meteor T.7	203 AFS
WL361/X-71	Meteor T.7	203 AFS
WH134	Meteor T.7	205 AFS
WH114/N-A	Meteor T.7	215 AFS
WG984/N-E	Meteor T.7	215 AFS
WG965	Meteor T.7	205 AFS
VW435	Meteor T.7	205 AFS
WG983/P-29	Meteor T.7	207 AFS
WA737/X-52	Meteor T.7	203 AFS
WL474/73	Meteor T.7	211 AFS
WL434/56	Meteor T.7	211 AFS
WL466/68	Meteor T.7	211 AFS
WH194/S-19	Meteor T.7	207 AFS
WA661/M-58	Meteor T.7	206 AFS
WG946/Y-72	Meteor T.7	206 AFS
WH228/46	Meteor T.7	209 AFS
WA712/42	Meteor T.7	209 AFS
2nd rank:		
TG622/A-C	Hastings MET.1	202 Sqdn
TG621/A-B	Hastings MET.1	202 Sqdn
WD500	Hastings C.4	24 Sqdn
WJ337/GAF	Hastings C.2	511 Sqdn
RF325/H-D	Lancaster MR.3	MRS
RE181/H-S	Lancaster MR.3	MRS
RE164/H-U	Lancaster MR.3	MRS
SW334/H-H	Lancaster MR.3	MRS
SX926	Lincoln B.2	61 Sqdn

RF448	Lincoln B.2	230 OCU
RE411	Lincoln B.2	100 Sqdn
RA665	Lincoln B.2	97 Sqdn
SX948	Lincoln B.2	527 Sqdn
RE311/48	Lincoln B.2	116 Sqdn
RE309/D	Lincoln B.2	CNCS
RF514/S	Lincoln B.2	CGS
3rd rank:		
EE349	Meteor F.3	29 MU
EE393	Meteor F.3	33 MU
EE359	Meteor F.3	33 MU
EE421	Meteor F.3	8 MU
EE339	Meteor F.3	29 MU
WA593	Meteor T.7	226 OCU
VW457	Meteor T.7	226 OCU
VW444/Y	Meteor T.7	228 OCU
VW456	Meteor T.7	226 OCU
VW454	Meteor T.7	ITS
WH450/A	Meteor F.8	500 Sqdn
WH451/G	Meteor F.8	500 Sqdn
WK742/F	Meteor F.8	601 Sqdn
WK722/A	Meteor F.8	601 Sqdn
WH359/K	Meteor F.8	611 Sqdn
VZ551/B	Meteor F.8	611 Sqdn
WH293/B	Meteor F.8	610 Sqdn
WH273/A	Meteor F.8	610 Sqdn
WH295/KQ-Q	Meteor F.8	226 OCU
WH308/KR-C	Meteor F.8	226 OCU
VZ522/WH-V	Meteor F.8	APS
WF686/Q	Meteor F.8	600 Sqdn
WH465/Y	Meteor F.8	600 Sqdn
WK692/F	Meteor F.8	604 Sqdn
WD645	Meteor NF.11	29 MU

7

Serial	Type	Unit
WM266	Meteor NF.11	15 MU
WM268	Meteor NF.11	15 MU
WM190	Meteor NF.11	33 MU
WM181	Meteor NF.11	33 MU
WM186	Meteor NF.11	33 MU
WM227/R	Meteor NF.11	228 OCU
WM265/F	Meteor NF.11	228 OCU
WM237/S	Meteor NF.11	228 OCU
WM152/G	Meteor NF.11	228 OCU
WM269/P	Meteor NF.11	228 OCU
WM233	Meteor NF.11	33 MU
WD633	Meteor NF.11	29 MU
WD632	Meteor NF.11	29 MU
WM244	Meteor NF.11	38 MU
WM257	Meteor NF.11	8 MU
WD592	Meteor NF.11	8 MU
WM234	Meteor NF.11	8 MU
WM229	Meteor NF.11	8 MU
WD634	Meteor NF.11	29 MU

4th rank:

Serial	Type	Unit
NZ5909	Bristol 170	41 Sqdn RNZAF
VX576	Valetta C.2	30 Sqdn
WJ475/D	Valetta T.3	1 ANS
WJ461/A	Valetta T.3	1 ANS
WJ477/Z	Valetta T.3	3 ANS
WJ468/B	Valetta T.3	2 ANS
WX522/B-N	Neptune MR.1	203 Sqdn
WX520/B-M	Neptune MR.1	203 Sqdn
WX518/B-J	Neptune MR.1	203 Sqdn
WX521/B-L	Neptune MR.1	203 Sqdn
WF429/K	Varsity T.1	2 ANS
WJ890/U	Varsity T.1	3 ANS
WF416/A	Varsity T.1	1 ANS
WL626/L	Varsity T.1	201 AFS
WJ939/Q	Varsity T.1	201 AFS
WJ568	Canberra B.2	57 Sqdn
WH856	Canberra B.2	10 Sqdn
WJ973	Canberra B.2	149 Sqdn
WE144	Canberra PR.3	540 Sqdn
WH673	Canberra B.2	RAFFC
WH639	Canberra B.2	RAFFC

RIGHT FLANK

1st (front) rank:

Serial	Type	Unit
WE326/A-A	Venom FB.1	266 Sqdn
WE327/A-L	Venom FB.1	266 Sqdn
WE331/A-B	Venom FB.1	266 Sqdn
WE330/A-S	Venom FB.1	266 Sqdn
XB582	Sabre F.4	3 Sqdn
XB684	Sabre F.4	3 Sqdn
XB705	Sabre F.4	67 Sqdn
XB626	Sabre F.4	67 Sqdn
WM676	Vampire NF.10	10 MU
WM703	Vampire NF.10	10 MU
WM677	Vampire NF.10	10 MU
WX215	Vampire FB.9	48 MU
WX224	Vampire FB.9	48 MU
WR265	Vampire FB.9	48 MU
WR258	Vampire FB.9	48 MU
WX213	Vampire FB.9	19 MU
VT822	Vampire F.3	19 MU
VF320	Vampire F.3	19 MU
VF340	Vampire F.3	19 MU
VV203	Vampire F.3	19 MU
VT806	Vampire F.3	19 MU
VT857	Vampire F.3	19 MU
VT871	Vampire F.3	19 MU
WB143/B-U	Meteor FR.9	2 Sqdn
VZ605/B-S	Meteor FR.9	2 Sqdn
VZ611/B-Z	Meteor FR.9	2 Sqdn
WH542/B-K	Meteor FR.9	2 Sqdn

2nd rank:

Serial	Type	Unit
WF545	Washington B.1	90 Sqdn
WF572/N	Washington B.1	35 Sqdn
WF562/K	Washington B.1	115 Sqdn
WF565	Washington B.1	207 Sqdn
WL747	Shackleton MR.2	269 Sqdn
WB828	Shackleton MR.1	CAPMF
WB824	Shackleton MR.1	CAPMF
WB819/B	Shackleton MR.1	269 Sqdn
TG560	Hastings C.1	116 Sqdn
WJ327	Hastings C.2	RAFFC

3rd rank:

Serial	Type	Unit
WR201	Vampire FB.9	27 MU
WR158	Vampire FB.9	48 MU
WR171	Vampire FB.9	27 MU
WR193	Vampire FB.9	10 MU
WR199	Vampire FB.9	10 MU
WR196	Vampire FB.9	10 MU
WR203	Vampire FB.9	27 MU
WR190	Vampire FB.9	27 MU
WR195	Vampire FB.9	10 MU
WR172	Vampire FB.9	27 MU
WR188	Vampire FB.9	48 MU
WA294/V9-C	Vampire FB.5	502 Sqdn
WG831/V9-H	Vampire FB.5	502 Sqdn
WA287	Vampire FB.5	233 OCU
WA362	Vampire FB.5	233 OCU
VZ812/LO-C	Vampire FB.5	602 Sqdn
WA137/LO-D	Vampire FB.5	602 Sqdn
VZ837/E	Vampire FB.5	614 Sqdn
WE837/D	Vampire FB.5	614 Sqdn
WA184/C	Vampire FB.5	614 Sqdn
WE836/B	Vampire FB.5	614 Sqdn
WG799/A	Vampire FB.5	614 Sqdn
VZ266/M	Vampire FB.5	614 Sqdn
VZ271/Q3-H	Vampire FB.5	613 Sqdn
VV616/Q3-K	Vampire FB.5	613 Sqdn
WA414/Q3-A	Vampire FB.5	613 Sqdn
VV602/Q3-B	Vampire FB.5	613 Sqdn
WA310	Vampire FB.5	233 OCU
VV689	Vampire FB.5	233 OCU

4th rank:

Serial	Type	Unit
VP975	Devon C.1	CCCS
VP966	Devon C.1	FTCCS
DF336	Oxford I	10 AFTS
PH521	Oxford I	9 AFTS
NM710/U-A	Oxford I	8 AFTS
X6781/S-P	Oxford I	8 AFTS
MP359/U-O	Oxford I	8 AFTS
HN203/N-Y	Oxford I	10 AFTS
DF418/M-X	Oxford I	10 AFTS
DF447/N-P	Oxford I	10 AFTS
NM309	Oxford I	9 AFTS
VL312/25	Anson C.19	527 Sqdn
VM313/34	Anson C.19	116 Sqdn
VV239/P	Anson T.21	1 ANS
WD421	Anson T.22	2 ASS
VV902/B	Anson T.21	CNCS
VV994/G	Anson T.21	6 ANS
VV976/P	Anson T.21	3 ANS
WZ551/36	Vampire T.11	208 AFS
WZ566/31	Vampire T.11	208 AFS
WZ570/N-50	Vampire T.11	202 AFS
WZ510	Vampire T.11	202 AFS
VV624/K	Vampire FB.5	CGS
VT830	Vampire F.3	19 MU

5th rank:

Serial	Type	Unit
WV783/F-X	Sycamore AS.12	ASWDU
XA302	Cadet TX.3	

CRESCENT

1st and 2nd ranks:

Serial	Type	Unit
WB550	Chipmunk T.10	22 MU
WB564	Chipmunk T.10	20 MU
WB573	Chipmunk T.10	22 MU
WB574/20	Chipmunk T.10	10 RFS
WB584	Chipmunk T.10	9 MU
WB610	Chipmunk T.10	22 MU
WB615	Chipmunk T.10	
WB619	Chipmunk T.10	20 MU
WB624	Chipmunk T.10	9 MU
WB627	Chipmunk T.10	20 MU
WB642	Chipmunk T.10	22 MU
WB643	Chipmunk T.10	20 MU
WB649	Chipmunk T.10	22 MU
WB659	Chipmunk T.10	22 MU
WB665	Chipmunk T.10	9 MU
WB666	Chipmunk T.10	20 MU
WB669	Chipmunk T.10	22 MU
WB687	Chipmunk T.10	22 MU
WB718	Chipmunk T.10	9 MU
WB752	Chipmunk T.10	9 MU
WB753	Chipmunk T.10	9 MU
WB763	Chipmunk T.10	9 MU
WG322/11	Chipmunk T.10	22 RFS
WG481	Chipmunk T.10	
WG487/16	Chipmunk T.10	9 RFS
WP835	Chipmunk T.10	5 RFS
WP909/20	Chipmunk T.10	Liverpool UAS
WP927	Chipmunk T.10	9 MU
WP929	Chipmunk T.10	10 MU
WP962	Chipmunk T.10	10 MU
WP965	Chipmunk T.10	9 MU
WP967	Chipmunk T.10	9 MU
WP968	Chipmunk T.10	9 MU
WP973	Chipmunk T.10	9 MU
WP976	Chipmunk T.10	9 MU
WP977	Chipmunk T.10	9 MU
WP978	Chipmunk T.10	10 MU
WP980	Chipmunk T.10	9 MU
WP981	Chipmunk T.10	9 MU
WP986	Chipmunk T.10	10 MU
WP987	Chipmunk T.10	10 MU
WP988	Chipmunk T.10	20 MU
WZ845/45	Chipmunk T.10	18 RFS
WZ846	Chipmunk T.10	20 MU

3rd rank:

Serial	Type	Unit
WZ865/JV	Chipmunk T.10	RAFC
WP865/JK	Chipmunk T.10	RAFC
WK559/DJ	Chipmunk T.10	RAFC
WP905/JR	Chipmunk T.10	RAFC
WP864/JJ	Chipmunk T.10	RAFC
KF755/O-T	Harvard IIB	CFS
KF372/P-P	Harvard IIB	3 FTS
FT214/P-B	Harvard IIB	3 FTS
KF466/Y-G	Harvard IIB	22 FTS
KF587/P-M	Harvard IIB	6 FTS
FT281/Q-D	Harvard IIB	6 FTS
KF165/O-E	Harvard IIB	6 FTS
KF702/M-Q	Harvard IIB	CFS
FT246/M-X	Harvard IIB	CFS
FT360/N-O	Harvard IIB	1 FTS
KF280/N-Q	Harvard IIB	1 FTS
FT245/N-A	Harvard IIB	CFS
WK558/DH	Chipmunk T.10	RAFC
WK565/DP	Chipmunk T.10	RAFC
WK554/DD	Chipmunk T.10	RAFC
WK568/DT	Chipmunk T.10	RAFC
WP857/JC	Chipmunk T.10	RAFC

4th rank:

Serial	Type	Unit
VF607/J	Auster AOP.6	664 Sqdn
VF515/T	Auster AOP.6	664 Sqdn
VF545/R	Auster AOP.6	664 Sqdn
WV427	Provost T.1	CFS
WV429	Provost T.1	CFS
VS689/M-L	Prentice T.1	2 FTS
VS628/N-J	Prentice T.1	CFS
VS319/N-I	Prentice T.1	CFS
VS733/N-B	Prentice T.1	CFS
VS641/M-F	Prentice T.1	1 FTS
VR273	Prentice T.1	1 FTS

VS411/M-M	Prentice T.1	1 FTS
VS684/M-J	Prentice T.1	1 FTS
VS270/B	Prentice T.1	1 ASS
VS364/Y-Z	Prentice T.1	22 FTS
VS259/M-E	Prentice T.1	3 FTS
VR245/N-B	Prentice T.1	3 FTS
WV434	Provost T.1	CFS
WV435	Provost T.1	CFS
VW985/D	Auster AOP.6	664 Sqdn
TW591/N	Auster AOP.6	664 Sqdn
TW582/M	Auster AOP.6	664 Sqdn

5th rank:

WZ848	Chipmunk T.10	20 MU
WZ849	Chipmunk T.10	20 MU
WZ850	Chipmunk T.10	10 MU
WG136/D-F	Balliol T.2	7 FTS
WG135/D-E	Balliol T.2	7 FTS
WG134/D-D	Balliol T.2	7 FTS
WG133/D-C	Balliol T.2	7 FTS
WG132/D-B	Balliol T.2	7 FTS
WG131/D-A	Balliol T.2	7 FTS
WZ851	Chipmunk T.10	10 MU
WZ852	Chipmunk T.10	20 MU
WZ857	Chipmunk T.10	10 MU

9 Right: *Part of the Varsity formation over Odiham on 15 July, taken from F/O Twigger's aircraft, WF334/U of 201 AFS. The tail of S/L Mott's WF387 can just be seen, further back is the other machine of the vic, WF412/H, flown by M/P OJ Thomas*

10 Below: *A mosaic made up of 4 photos taken on 5 July by the School of Aerial Photography. Note that there is still some tidying up of the Washingtons, Shackletons and Bristol Freighter needing to be done*

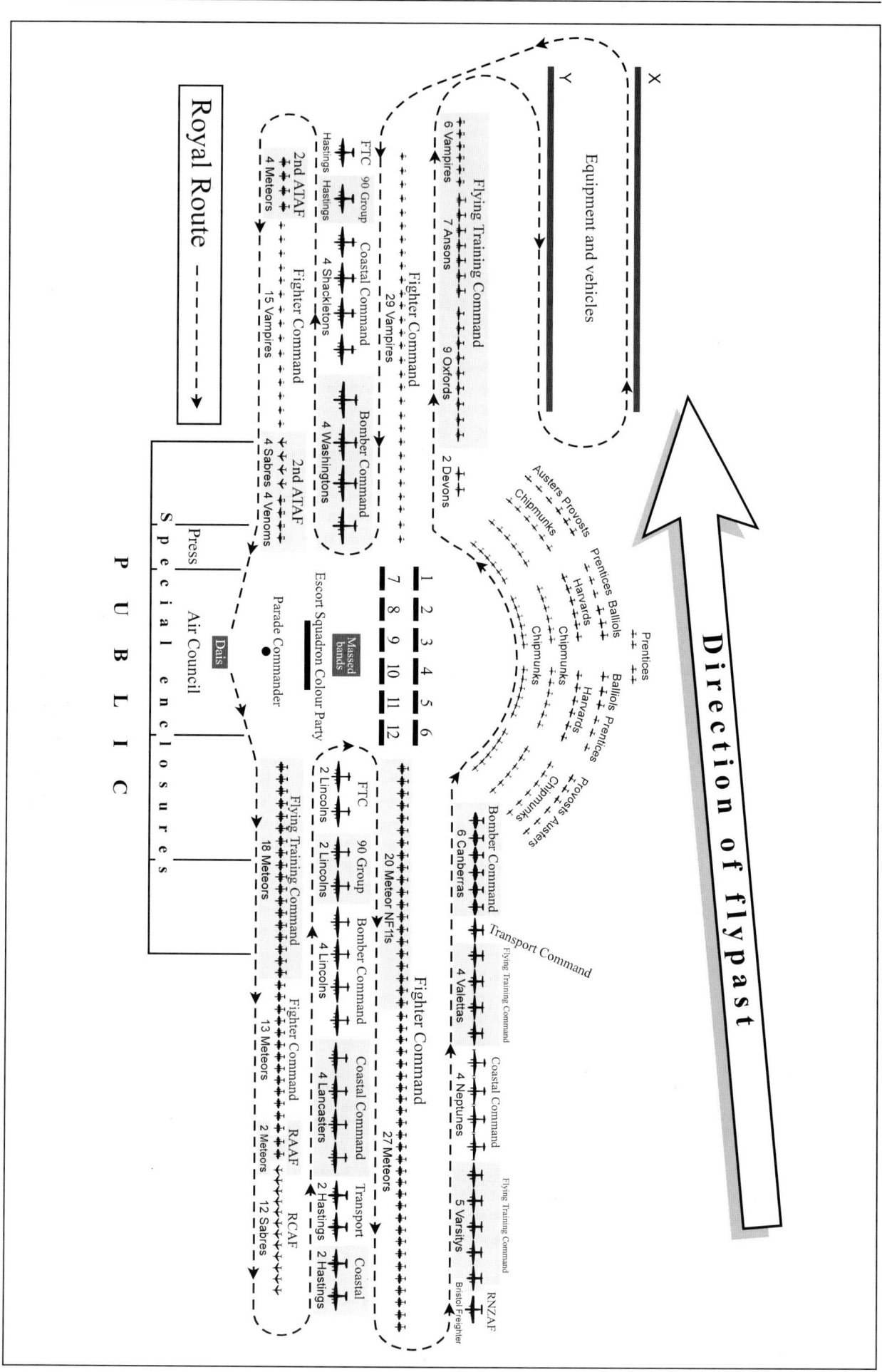

11: Bright yellow Bristol Sycamore HR.12, WV783/F-X, of the ASWDU. Note the Westland hydraulic winch near the rotor head

12: DHC Chipmunk T.10 WB550 of 22 MU

13: Pristine North American Harvard IIB, KF165/O-E, of 6 Flying Training School. Note the unit badge

14: A rather high contrast shot of Hunting Percival Provost T.1, WV427 of the Central Flying School. The school's pelican badge can be clearly seen on the engine cowling

15: Airspeed Oxford I, X6781/S-P, of 8 Air Flying Training School

16: Avro Anson C.19, VL312/25, of 527 Squadron with the unit emblem clearly visible on the rudder

17: Boulton Paul Balliol T.2, WG131, of 7 Flying Training School

18: Vickers Valetta C.2, VX576, of 30 Squadron. Note the early Transport Command titling on a white cheat line, just visible on the fuselage

19: This is the sole Bristol 170 Freighter to take part in the Review. Exceptionally shiny, NZ5909 of 41 Squadron RNZAF, was one of several used by the Royal New Zealand Air Force. Of interest are the glazed panels in the nose and the enormous fin flash

20: Avro Lincoln B.2, RE411 of 100 Squadron, wearing the immediate post-war heavy night bomber camouflage of Medium Sea Grey and Gloss Black. There are numerous small stencil markings scattered about the fuselage. Lincoln B.2, RA665 of 97 Squadron, can be made out in the background

21: Avro Lincoln B.2, RE309/D, of the Central Navigation and Control School. The dull finish is enlivened by a yellow fuselage band. For some reason the fuselage radome on this aircraft is grey rather than the more common black

22: Boeing Washington B.1, WF572/N, of 35 Squadron. Note how all the propeller blades are 'at attention', the pull ropes for the chocks are laid out parallel to the wings, and even the bombs and bomb trolley have been bulled up for the event

23: Looking pristine in white and grey, this is Avro Lancaster MR.3, RE164/H-U, of the Maritime Reconnaissance School, built as one of the last batches of Lancasters. Many were completed as Lincolns

24: *Avro Lancaster MR.3, SW334/H-H, of the Maritime Reconnaissance School. Many of the late-production Lancasters were diverted to Coastal Command as the war finished, SW334 among them. With hindsight, perhaps the anti-U-boat campaign would have been over quicker if more had been used for this purpose earlier in the conflict*

25: *Son of Lancaster? This is Avro Shackleton MR.2 WL747 of 269 Squadron. Sometimes described as "10,000 rivets in formation", the type had a long and honourable career lasting over 30 years*

26: *Contrasting greatly with other maritime aircraft in its Sea Blue finish, this is Lockheed Neptune MR.1, WX521/B-L, of 203 Squadron. The RAF later standardised on four-engined aircraft for its maritime reconnaissance role*

27 Top left: *A closeup of the nose of one of the two Avro Shackleton MR.1s of the CAPMF in the static display. Note the Coastal Command emblem on the nose*

28 Lower left: *A Shackleton MR.1 looms over the Vampire F.3s of 19 MU*

29 Right: *Handley Page Hastings Met.1, TG622/A-C, of 202 Squadron in Medium Sea Grey finish with red codes*

30: *A study in tails in the second rank, right flank of the static display. The red tail belongs to Hastings C.2 WJ327 of the RAFFC. Next is a Hastings C.1, TG560 of 116 Squadron, closely followed by three Shackleton MR.1s (WB819/B, WB824 and WB828) and a single MR.2 (WL747). Dominating the skyline are four Washington B.1s, the nearest being WF565 of 207 Squadron*

31: *Handley Page Hastings C.(VIP), WD500, of 24 Squadron. Note the distinctive cheat line and anti-glare panel*

32: *A fuller view of Hastings C.2 WJ327 of the Royal Air Force Flying College. It is finished in what was the standard colour scheme for the type at the time, but with the addition of a red tail fin and wing tips*

33 Above: *Members of the public showing how small Vampire FB.9, WR196 of 10 MU really was—and Washington WF572/N of 35 Squadron wasn't*

34 Left: *De Havilland Vampire T.11, WZ566/31 of 208 Advanced Flying School*

35: *Vampire T.11 WZ570/N-50 of 202 Advanced Flying School. Finish is all-silver enlivened by broad yellow bands around the tail booms and wings*

36: De Havilland Vampire FB.5, WE837/D, of 614 Auxiliary Air Force Squadron, proudly displaying its red and green triangle markings on the fuselage booms. These were inspired by the red dragon and green hills of Wales where the squadron was based

37: Vampire FB.5, VZ271/Q3-H, of 613 Squadrons. This unit has adopted full codes rather than the decorative bars flanking the boom roundels, but it does carry the squadron bage on the nose

38: Vampire FB.5, WA294/V9-C, of 502 Squadron. The three Washingtons in the background (WF562/K, WF572/N AND WF545) belong to 115, 35 and 90 Squadrons respectively

19

39: *Vampire FB.5, WA294/V9-C, of 502 Squadron displays another variation of unit markings. This aircraft carries both code letters and a small representation of the blue band with red lightning flash adopted as an identity marking*

40: *De Havilland Venom FB.1 WE326/A-A of 236 (Rhodesia) Squadron from 2nd TAF shows the return of camouflage and a legend on the tip tank which reads 'Hlabezulu'. This is the squadron motto and originated from the unit's African connections*

41: *What the crowd saw at ground level. These are the Meteor T.7s of 211 Advanced Flying School, WL434/56 being the nearest. Note the Fleet Air Arm pilot*

42 Above: Dwarfed by the balloon and basket used for parachute training, Vampire F.3 VT830 belongs to 19 MU, while FB.5, VV624/K is from the Central Gunnery School

43 Right: One of the many silver Meteor F.8s displaying bright fuselage markings, this is WH451/G of 500 Squadron

44 Right: By way of contrast, this is how many Meteors looked in later years. WH450/A of 500 Squadron took part in the static display but not wearing these colours. The rising tensions of the Cold War prompted a return to camouflage for the RAF's fighters, but unit pride retained the colourful fuselage markings

21

45: *This is Meteor F.8, VZ522/WH-V, of the Armament Practice Station in trainer silver with a yellow fuselage band*

46: *Meteor F.8 WK943/N of 257 Squadron sporting yellow and green checks on its fuselage*

47: *Gloster Meteor F.8 WK722A of 601 (County of London) Squadron, RAuxAF. The red and black triangles on the fuselage are matched by the tail stripes which identify it as the CO's aircraft. Note the unit emblem on the engine nacelle and the ready-use fire extinguisher in the foreground*

48: Meteor F.8 WH465/Y of 600 Squadron, RAuxAF. The markings flanking the roundel consisted of red and white triangles

49: Displaying what were possibly the most colourful squadron markings of all, consisting of red and yellow triangles on a black bar, this is Gloster Meteor F.8, WH359/K, of 611 Squadron

50: Gloster Meteor F.8 WK692/F of 604 Squadron. The unit fuselage markings are red and golden yellow

51: The men of 610 Squadron RAuxAF must have been very proud of of their aircraft, as Meteor F.8 WH293/B not only carries the black and white unit markings on the fuselage, it also has a miniature version flanking the unit crest on the engine nacelle

52: Meteor F.8 WK658/G of 63 Squadron, complete with black and yellow fuselage markings

53: Looking very dull compared to the operational versions, this is Gloster Meteor T.7, WG946/Y-72 of 206 Advanced Flying School. Behind is a Lincoln B.2, RF514/S, of the Central Gunnery School

54 Right: *Side view of Gloster Meteor FR.9 WH542/B-K of 2 Squadron. The camouflage gives it a much more purposeful appearance than the all-silver pure fighters. Note the Staffordshire knot unit emblem on the engine nacelle*

55 Below: *A head-on view of Gloster Meteor FR.9 WH542/B-K of 2 Squadron. The glazed panels over the nose-mounted cameras are readily apparent, as are the four gun ports. Immaculate Hastings C.2, WJ327 of the RAFFC, towers overhead*

56 Right: *Gloster Meteor trainer F.3, EE359, was one of the older versions of the type on display. It was serving with 33 Maintenance Unit. It also served with the Empire Flying School and 616 Squadron*

57 Above: *Tail study 1. A lineup of Meteor T.7s from various Advanced Flying Schools. WA712 and WH228 being from 209, WG946 from 206*

58 Left: *Meteor NF.11 WM237/S of No. 228 Operational Conversion Unit*

59 Left: *Tail study 2 showing the distinctive swept fins of the Canadair-built Sabre F.2s of the Royal Canadian Air Force. The four nearest are from 439 Squadron, while the black and white chevrons identify machines from 410 Squadron. Further back still are the striped fins of 441 Squadron. On the left are the Hastings of 24 and 202 Squadrons of the RAF*

60: *Colourful Canadair Sabre F.2 19159/AM-159 of 410 'Cougar' Squadron, RCAF. The Canadians were more exuberant in the treatment of their aircraft, perhaps picking up the habit from their neighbours to the south. The unit emblem is visible below the canopy*

61: *BT151 is another Sabre 2, serial number 19151, and carries the identity markings of 441 Squadron RCAF. These three Canadian Sabre squadrons made up No.1 Wing RCAF, and during their stay in Britain created regular sonic booms, to the apparent satisfaction of several Members of Parliament—a possibly different reaction to today*

62: *A full view of Sabre 19192 of 439 Squadron RCAF, whose sabre-toothed tiger fin decoration seems very apt on a Sabre 2*

63: The RAF Sabres carried an altogether more business-like finish than their Canadian counterparts. This is F.4, XB626 of 67 Squadron

64: XB582 is another Sabre F.4, this one being in service with 3 Squadron. Note the extensive stencilling

65: XB705 was the second of two Sabres 4s from 67 Squadron on display in the static park

66: English Electric Canberra PR.3, WE144, of 540 Squadron

67: English Electric Canberra B.2, WH639, in service with the RAF Flying College. Behind are the rows of Chipmunks on the crescent

68: Formation 39 consisting of 24 Canberras from Binbrook passing overhead at 1,100 feet at 300 knots/345 mph

Lunchtime flyovers:

De Havilland DH.82 Tiger Moth, G-AHUT, flown by CCF Cadet Q. Oswell on his first solo cross-country flight from Fairoaks.
North American Harvard IIB, FX283/X-O, of 6 FTS, flown by Acting P/O C. Beadle.
Gloster Meteor T.7, WL368/W, of the Instrument Training School, West Raynham.
English Electric Canberra PR.3, WE137, of 540 Squadron.
Handley Page Hastings MET.1, TG567/A-G, of 202 Squadron.

The next item should have comprised two Meteor FR.9s from Stradishall, but radio problems prevented a successful run.
Supermarine Spitfire LF.16E, TE389/C, from 1 CAACU, Hornchurch.
Auster AOP.6, VF543, of 662 Squadron.
Handley Page Hastings C.2, WD499, of RAFFC, flown by W/C WJ Burnett and Air Commodore SR Ubee returning from a flight over the North Pole.
English Electric Canberra PR.3, WE141, of 540 Squadron returning from Malta.
Handley Page Hastings C.2, WD475/G, of 47 Squadron, returning on a CASEVAC flight from Korea.

THE FLYPAST
Formations and their aircraft

In the boxes which follow (all in their Flypast order), the relative positions of the aircraft in the formations are as viewed from above, with the leader at the top. They may not be entirely correct for all formations as the Bentley Priory records contain a mixture of conventions. Since enthusiasts' records for the Lincoln formations appear to contain some aircraft which only took part in rehearsals (53 serials for only 45 aircraft!), no data from that source has been used for any of the Flypast formations except for the Hastings. The aircraft serial and code details listed are all as received from the pilots' log books unless a note appears indicating another source (occasionally photographs or Form 541s). Unit details refer to the aircrew involved; the aircraft belonged to the same unit unless otherwise noted. For more details of serial-to-code tie-ups, refer to the table on page 91.

As the tour of inspection by the Royal party ended, the CFE Venoms returned to sky-write 'ER':

69 Above: 11 Vampire FB.5s and a solitary Vampire T.11 (WZ561) of the FTC during rehearsals on 11 July. All wear silver finish with yellow training bands around the booms

70 Left: HRH Queen Elizabeth II and HRH The Duke of Edinburgh taking the salute during the march past by the Parade either shortly before lunch at 12.35, or later again at 14.30. Following an inspection of the Static Parade, the flypast was scheduled to begin at 15.40. Standing behind the Duke and saluting is the Chief of Air Staff, ACM Sir WF Dickson

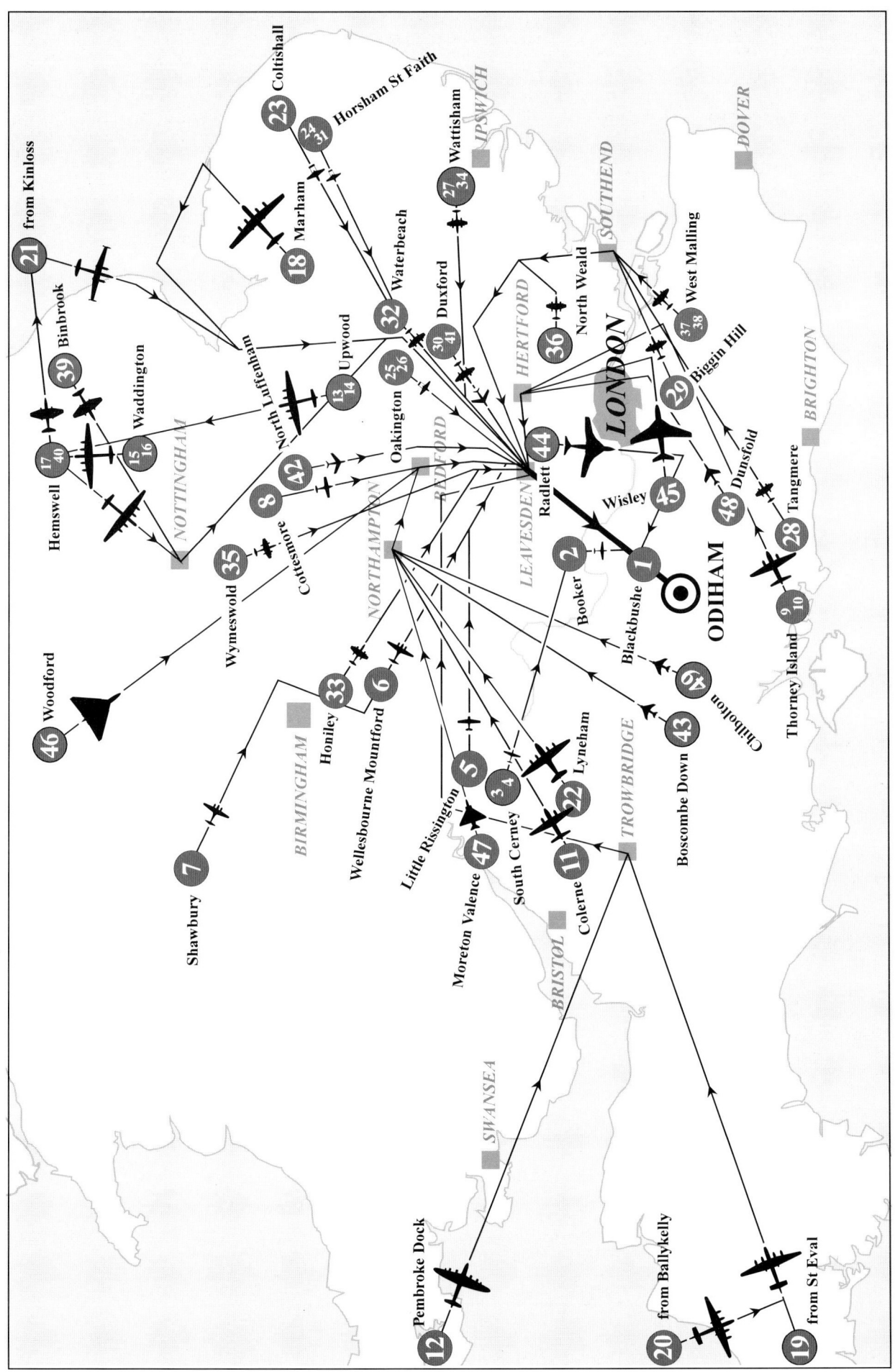

THE SKYWRITING VENOMS

CFE West Raynham
4 Venom FB.1s operated from Farnborough

The Flypast proceedings proper then commenced with a single Sycamore trailing the RAF Ensign:

FORMATION 1

Fighter Command
275 Squadron
Sycamore HR 13, XD196, operated from Blackbushe
Time over Odiham: 15.39.5
Altitude: 800 feet
Speed: 86 mph/75 knots

Notes: The official RAF report on the Review numbers the first 7 formations as 1A, 1B, 2A, 2B, 3, 4A and 4B. To avoid confusion, formations in this book have been numbered consecutively.

The Flypast actually began 30 seconds earlier than scheduled

71 Left: The RAF College Chipmunk formation over the clock tower of RAF Cranwell on their return after the review

72 Right: DHC Chipmunk T.10, WZ865/JV, of the RAF College, Cranwell, parked among many others of the same type on the crescent during the display. The college badge is clearly visible on the engine cowling

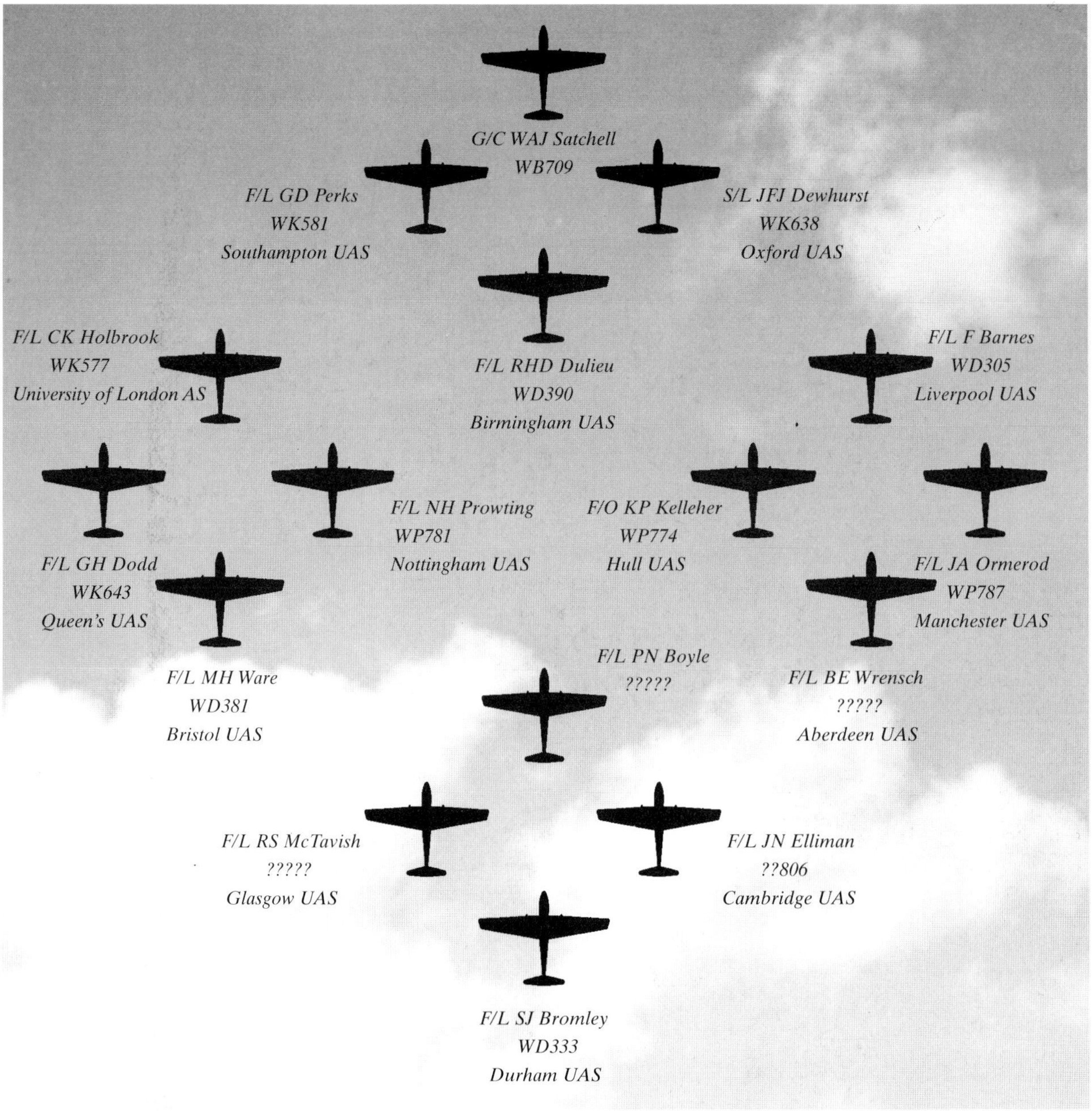

G/C WAJ Satchell
WB709

F/L GD Perks
WK581
Southampton UAS

S/L JFJ Dewhurst
WK638
Oxford UAS

F/L CK Holbrook
WK577
University of London AS

F/L RHD Dulieu
WD390
Birmingham UAS

F/L F Barnes
WD305
Liverpool UAS

F/L GH Dodd
WK643
Queen's UAS

F/L NH Prowting
WP781
Nottingham UAS

F/O KP Kelleher
WP774
Hull UAS

F/L JA Ormerod
WP787
Manchester UAS

F/L MH Ware
WD381
Bristol UAS

F/L PN Boyle
?????

F/L BE Wrensch
?????
Aberdeen UAS

F/L RS McTavish
?????
Glasgow UAS

F/L JN Elliman
??806
Cambridge UAS

F/L SJ Bromley
WD333
Durham UAS

FORMATION 2

Home Command
16 DHC Chipmunk T.10s operated from Booker
Time over Odiham: 15.40
Altitude: 1,100 feet
Speed: 98 mph/85 knots

Notes:
BBC Commentator Cliff Michelmore flew with either F/L Ormerod or F/L Barnes.

The only possible aircraft for F/L Elliman is WP806 which, from the record card, was on charge with 15 RFS.

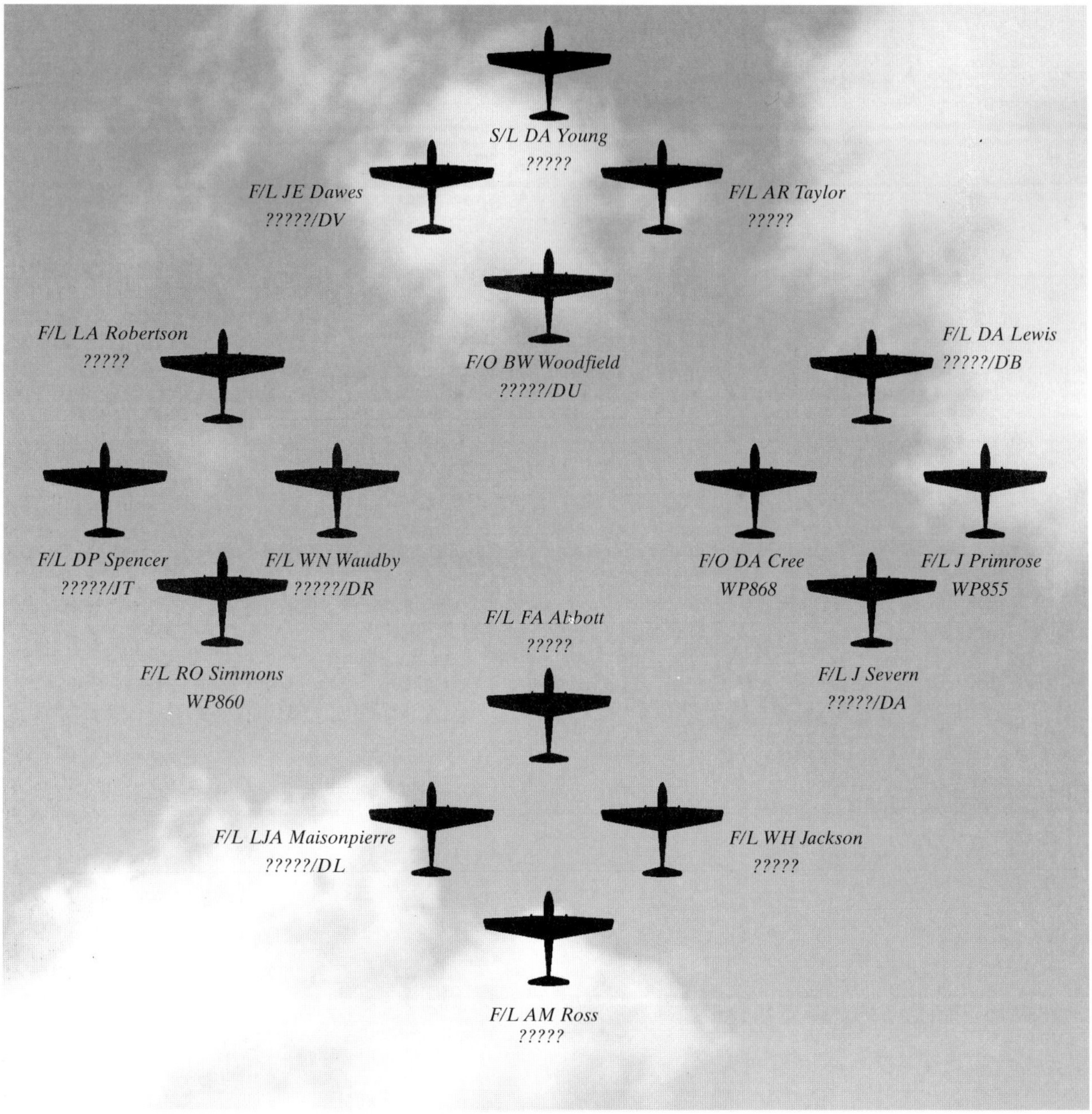

S/L DA Young
?????

F/L JE Dawes
?????/DV

F/L AR Taylor
?????

F/L LA Robertson
?????

F/O BW Woodfield
?????/DU

F/L DA Lewis
?????/DB

F/L DP Spencer
?????/JT

F/L WN Waudby
?????/DR

F/O DA Cree
WP868

F/L J Primrose
WP855

F/L RO Simmons
WP860

F/L FA Abbott
?????

F/L J Severn
?????/DA

F/L LJA Maisonpierre
?????/DL

F/L WH Jackson
?????

F/L AM Ross
?????

FORMATION 3

Flying Training Command
16 DHC Chipmunk T.10s from the RAF College operated from South Cerney

Time over Odiham: 15.40-50
Altitude: 1,200 feet
Speed: 98 mph/85 knots

73 Left: Coded 'DM' Chipmunk T.10, WK562. was in service with the RAF College in July 1953 and may well have taken part in the Review flypast. It is seen here being flown by the author with 10 AEF over Woodvale in February 1992

```
                        S/L EC Gartrell
                            ?????
                           CFS (B)

  F/L BN Byrne & F/L Davies              F/L GD Bain
           VS627                          ?????/N-X
          CFS (B)                          CFS (B)
                        F/L P Thomas
                         ?????/N-T
                          CFS (B)

         F/L KJ Evans                  S/L MG Crotty
            ?????                        ?????/N-F
           22 FTS                         3 FTS

F/L GG Dillingham   F/O DF Shaw   F/O WS Jacques &        F/O RE Mackie
    ?????/YA          ?????        F/L R Maclachlan         ?????/N-L
    22 FTS           22 FTS          ?????/N-N                3 FTS
                                      3 FTS
         F/L JH Kingsbury              F/L DW Swart
           VS393/Z-O                    ?????/N-R
            22 FTS                       3 FTS
```

FORMATION 4

Flying Training Command

12 Percival Prentice T.1s from CFS (B) based at South Cerney; 3 FTS based at Feltwell and 22 FTS at Syerston. All operated from South Cerney

Time over Odiham: 15.41
Altitude: 1,000 feet
Speed: 98 mph/85 knots

Note: The record card for VS627 states that it was with the CFS until 18 June 1953 then went to 29 MU as surplus to requirements

There was much agonising over the approach route to Odiham which infringed on the traffic patterns of both Heathrow and Northolt. Objections by the Civil Aviation authorities were overruled on account of the flypast passing the Queen at an unacceptable angle.

Weather considerations determined that the flypast would consist of a parade of 12 and 24 aircraft formations. Two alternative forms were planned: Plan 'A' for good weather, Plan 'B' for cloud conditions with lower altitudes for heavy aircraft. On the day Plan 'B' was used.

15 rehearsals were flown, although 20 were planned.

Distances from the Royal Dais were planned to give an easy viewing angle for the Queen, viz: helicopter 400 yards out; light aircraft at 1,000 and 1,200 feet—600 yards out; all other aircraft except Canberras—800 yards out; Canberras—1,000 yards out.

On Review Day the average time error between formations was 4.5 seconds.

74 : The Queen and the Duke of Edinburgh clearly enjoying themselves during the flypast

75 Left: *15.42—twelve radial engines in formation as the Harvards take their noisy bow*

FORMATION 5

Flying Training Command
12 North American Harvard IIBs from CFS (A) based at Little Rissington; 1 FTS based at Moreton-in-the-Marsh and 6 FTS at Ternhill. All operated from Little Rissington

Time over Odiham: 15.41.50
Altitude: 1,200 feet
Speed: 138 mph/120 knots

Note: The logbook records for the serials show only the numbers. The letters are deduced from the record card tie-up with the unit concerned

Serial/code tie-ups (from the Air Britain Harvard File) are:
CFS (A): FX252/M-W, KF150/N-T, KF172/N-W
1 FTS: KF487/N-T, KF748/N-U
6 FTS: KF730/P-Z

76: *W/C CLW Stewart leading the Oxfords of Flying Training Command*

W/C CLW Stewart
LX687
9 AFTS

F/O EL Simmonds
PH424
9 AFTS

F/L DM Howarth
DF463
9 AFTS

F/L RD Campbell
HN585
8 AFTS

F/L NH Frost
NM276
9 AFTS

F/L NF Brown
PG978
10 AFTS

F/O JCL Ainger
HM751
8 AFTS

F/L JW Peckowski
P8995
8 AFTS

F/O HR Lane
P8978
10 AFTS

F/S RF Berners
DF346
10 AFTS

F/O HG Haines
X6862
8 AFTS

F/O TJ Pugh
NM245
10 AFTS

FORMATION 6

Flying Training Command

12 Airspeed Oxford Is from 9 AFTS based at Wellesbourne Mountford, 8 AFTS based at Dalcross and 10 AFTS based at Pershore. All operated from Wellesbourne Mountford

Time over Odiham: 15.42
Altitude: 1,100 feet
Speed: 138 mph/120 knots

Notes: The serials are confirmed from a photo taken on the 15th July, and all but DF463, DF346 and NM245 are also confirmed from pilots' logbooks

HM723 had a major accident when it struck the ground due to turbulence in a stream landing at Wellesbourne Mountford after one of the rehearsals. The pilot, F/O Haines, was unhurt

From a photo in F/O Lane's logbook, P8978 was coded O-Z

F/L G Powell
VV975
CNCS
F/S AB Howes
VV881
CNCS
F/O WHE Michelin
VV331
CNCS
F/S Coulbeck
?????
CNCS
F/L EW Poole
WJ549/J
6 ANS
F/L Banfield
WD435/A
1 ASS
F/S J Tichy
WJ548/T
6 ANS
F/S RB Smith
VS576/F
6 ANS
F/O H McC Vincent
WD433
1 ASS
F/O J Cookson
WD434
1 ASS
F/O WO Lewis
?????
6 ANS
F/O Lawrence
?????
1 ASS

A
WD435

WG134
D
D

FORMATION 7

Flying Training Command

12 Avro Anson T.21and T.22s from CNCS based at Shawbury, 6 ANS based at Lichfield and 1 ASS based at Swanton Morley. All operated from Shawbury

Time over Odiham: 15.42 50
Altitude: 1,200 feet
Speed: 138 mph/120 knots

Notes: *The serials come from the Bentley Priory record. Only WD435 is confirmed from the pilot's logbook*
F/O Lewis's aircraft was probably VS578 (author's records)

77: *Avro Anson T.22 WD435 of 1 ASS flown by F/L Banfield*

78: *Balliol T.2, WG134/D-D, of 7 FTS seen on the rear rank of the crescent*

79 Right: *Balliol T.2s of 7 FTS seen from F/S Cover's aircraft*

W/C G McKenzie
F/L RG Lofting
?????/P-R

F/L AD Mercer
WG118/Q-X

S/L E Stephenson
F/L AC Burn
?????/P-P

F/L RA Gillam
WG112/Q-T

S/L RWW James
WG179

F/L EG Beedle
?????

M/P A Wiseman
?????

F/O PH Salter
?????

F/S AE Cover
WG120/D-Q

F/JR Powell
WG124

M/P KF Scott
?????/Q-S

Sgt HW Gibson
?????

FORMATION 8

Flying Training Command
12 Boulton Paul Balliol T.2s from 7 FTS Cottesmore, operated from Cottesmore

Time over Odiham: 15.43
Altitude: 1,100 feet
Speed: 166 mph/145 knots

Note: A photo taken on 15 July confirms 'P-R' and WG118/Q-X. It also shows that the No. 4 in the lead box is WG112/Q-T, whereas F/L Gillam's logbook records WG141. It may be that F/L Gillam flew in one of the other boxes, and not as shown on the Bentley Priory record

FORMATION 9

Flying Training Command
6 Vickers Varsity T.1s from 2 ANS based at Thorney Island, and 3 ANS based at Bishops Court. All operated from Thorney Island

Time over Odiham: 15.43 50
Altitude: 1,500 feet
Speed: 166 mph 145 knots

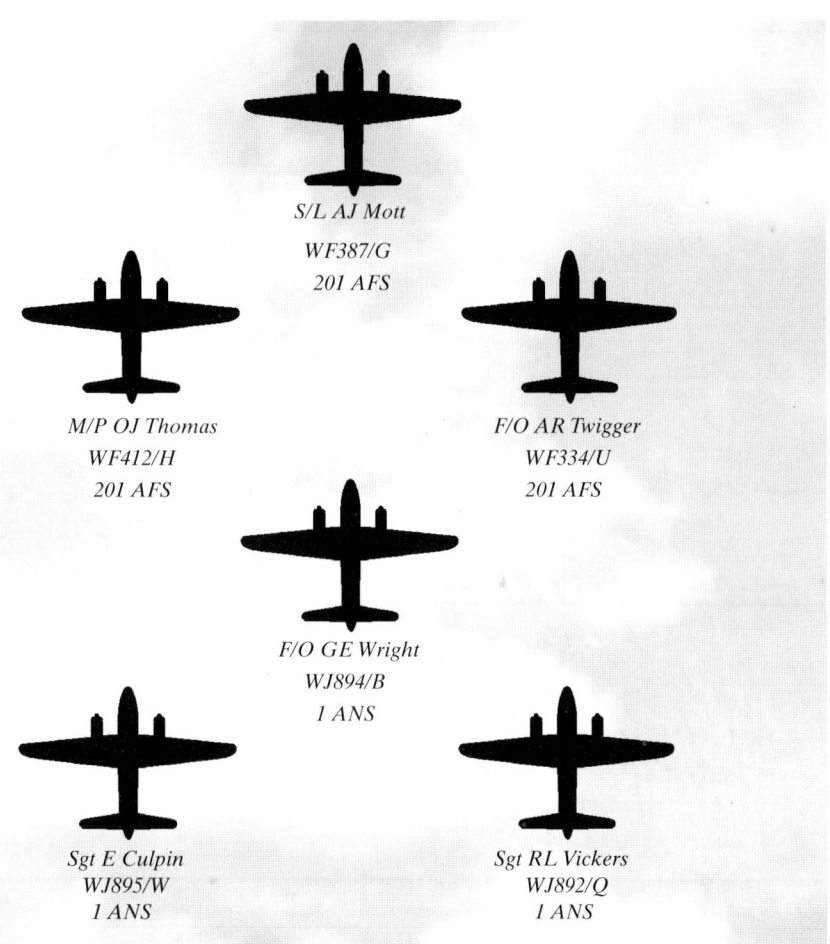

F/L A Gavan
WJ886/O
2 ANS

F/O SF Fraze
WJ903
2 ANS

Sgt NE Hollins
WJ891
2 ANS

F/L GA Hamilton
WF421
3 ANS

F/S K Miture
WJ905
3 ANS

F/O PF Wilson
WF422
3 ANS

FORMATION 10

Flying Training Command
6 Vickers Varsity T.1s from 201 AFS based at Swinderby and 1 ANS based at Hullavington. All operated from Thorney Island

Time over Odiham: 15.44
Altitude: 1,100 feet
Speed: 166 mph/145 knots

Note: The above serials come from the Bentley Priory record. All are confirmed by photos taken on 15 July

S/L AJ Mott
WF387/G
201 AFS

M/P OJ Thomas
WF412/H
201 AFS

F/O AR Twigger
WF334/U
201 AFS

F/O GE Wright
WJ894/B
1 ANS

Sgt E Culpin
WJ895/W
1 ANS

Sgt RL Vickers
WJ892/Q
1 ANS

80: Vickers Varsity T.1, WF249/K, of 2 Air Navigation School. Just visible behind is Varsity T.1, WJ890/U, of 3 ANS

81: This is Valetta WJ461/A, of 1 ANS. Note how the aircraft identity letter is repeated on the nose and the squadron emblem just behind the cockpit

FORMATION 11

Transport/Maintenance Command

6 Vickers Valetta C.1/T.3s from 242 OCU, 39 MU, 30 and 167 Squadrons. All operated from Colerne

Time over Odiham: 15.44 50
Altitude: 1,500 feet
Speed: 166 mph/145 knots

Note: *The serials are from the pilots' logbooks. A photo taken on 15 July shows the code for S/L Taylor's aircraft, and that F/L Elliot's aircraft was coded 'QO-E'. Enthusiasts' records give VW864 as the serial for the code 'NU-L'*

S/L EH Taylor
?????/NU-L
242 OCU

F/L JH Elliot
VX484
167 Squadron

F/O B D'Oliviera
VW842
30 Squadron

F/L JH Spurgeon & A P/O BJ King
WJ466
39 MU

F/L JS Luby
WJ482
39 MU

F/L DE Walton
WJ480
39 MU

82: *The Valetta formation trundles overhead at 166 mph, S/L EH Taylor of 242 OCU in NU-L at the front*

83: *One of the rarest sights of all—three majestic flying boats in formation. These are the Sunderlands of 230 Squadron, led by S/L Higgins in RN270*

FORMATION 12

Coastal Command
3 Short Sunderland Vs from 230 Squadron, operated from Pembroke Dock

Time over Odiham: 15.45
Altitude: 1,600 feet
Speed: 150 mph/130 knots

Note: *The Form 541 record is confirmed by a photo taken on 15 July*

S/L JS Higgins
RN270/B-O

S/L CM Cassels
SZ581/B-Y

S/L CM Stavert
ML763/B-R

FORMATION 13

Bomber Command
9 Avro Lincoln B.2s from 214, 7 and 148 Squadrons, operated from Upwood

Time over Odiham: 15.45 75
Altitude: 1,100 feet
Speed: 166 mph/150 knots

Notes: Serials all come from the Form 541 record. All aircraft in this formation are confirmed from photos taken on 15 July

During rehearsals the Lincoln formations had some difficulty in formation-keeping, partly because of their small reserves of power and partly as the wish of Bomber Command to fly with three aircraft in vic with sections also in vic. This type of formation was subsequently changed to sections in line astern and on the Review Day the result was an excellent standard of formation-keeping by the Lincolns

S/L EP Landon
SX958
214 Squadron

F/O AA Ramus
SX975
214 Squadron

F/L WH Burden
RE360
214 Squadron

S/L DC Saunders
RE301
7 Squadron

F/S JE Sowerby
SX982
7 Squadron

F/S KS Kijak
SX988
7 Squadron

S/L SC Dunmore
RE397
148 Squadron

F/S CG Hodkinson
SX983
148 Squadron

F/O KG Dougan
SX987
148 Squadron

FORMATION 14

Bomber Command
9 Avro Lincoln B.2s from 214, 7 and 148 Squadrons, operated from Upwood

Time over Odiham: 15.46:50
Altitude: 1,600 feet
Speed: 166 mph/150 knots

Notes: *Serials all come from the Form 541 record. RA673 is confirmed from the pilot's logbook*

F/L PNB Pritchett
RA673
148 Squadron

F/L PJ Whittacker
RA664
148 Squadron

F/S W Szmaciarz
RE347
148 Squadron

Sgt AJM Merry
RE400
7 Squadron

F/O DS Emsley
RE362
7 Squadron

F/O JB Stephens
RE345
7 Squadron

F/O PR Watson
RA709
214 Squadron

F/S A Ross
RE299
214 Squadron

F/S WDE Martin
RE295
7 Squadron

FORMATION 15

Bomber Command

9 Avro Lincoln B.2s from 61 and 49 Squadrons, operated from Waddington

Time over Odiham: 15.47 25
Altitude: 1,100 feet
Speed: 166 mph/150 knots

Notes: *Serials all come from the Form 541 record.*

RA681 belonged to the Reserve Holding Unit at Waddington

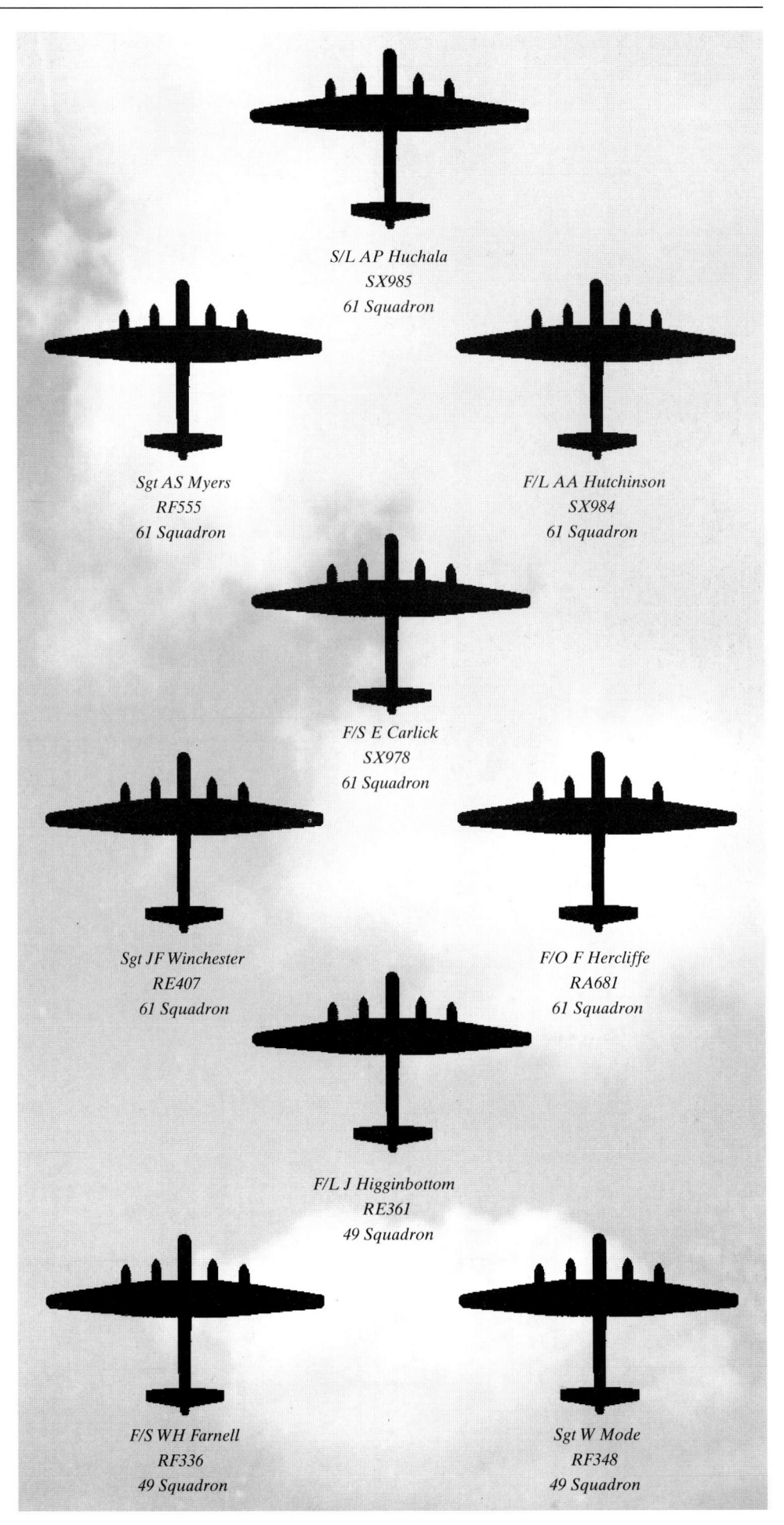

S/L AP Huchala
SX985
61 Squadron

Sgt AS Myers
RF555
61 Squadron

F/L AA Hutchinson
SX984
61 Squadron

F/S E Carlick
SX978
61 Squadron

Sgt JF Winchester
RE407
61 Squadron

F/O F Hercliffe
RA681
61 Squadron

F/L J Higginbottom
RE361
49 Squadron

F/S WH Farnell
RF336
49 Squadron

Sgt W Mode
RF348
49 Squadron

45

FORMATION 16

Bomber Command

9 Avro Lincoln B.2s from 49 and 100 Squadrons, operated from Waddington

Time over Odiham: 15.48
Altitude: 1,600 feet
Speed: 166 mph/150 knots

Notes: Serials all come from the Form 541 record. SX989 is confirmed from the pilot's logbook

*Many enthusiasts' records quote SS716 and WD148 as taking part. The first machine flew on most of the rehearsals up to 10 July, but not afterwards. F/O Delaney had to feather No. 1 engine on his first aircraft; he landed and was airborne in SX979 fifteen minutes after the rest of the formation. Although no serial is mentioned for the faulty aircraft, it may have been WD148

SX989 belonged to the Reserve Holding Unit at Waddington

S/L RI Alexander
SX944
100 Squadron

F/S V Ryba
RF335
100 Squadron

S/L AE Newitt
RF349
49 Squadron

*F/O D Delaney**
SX979
100 Squadron

F/S K Zmitrowicz
SX989
49 Squadron

F/L JA Worrall
RE359
49 Squadron

F/L GM Bailey
SX933
100 Squadron

P/O EE Fell
RA714
100 Squadron

F/O R Shilton
SX937
100 Squadron

FORMATION 17

Bomber Command
9 Avro Lincoln B.2s from 83 and 97 Squadrons, operated from Hemswell

Time over Odiham: 15.48 75
Altitude: 1,100 feet
Speed: 166 mph/150 knots

Notes: *Serials all come from the Form 541 record*

S/L WC Sinclair
RF575
83 Squadron

F/S J Kmiecik
RA693
83 Squadron

Capt FF Hamilton
RA677
83 Squadron

F/L KP Souter
RA672
83 Squadron

Sgt EW Quinney
RE415
83 Squadron

F/L JSF Blundell
RE358
83 Squadron

F/L JA Williams
RA713/B
97 Squadron

Sgt KE Fluck
RF574/V
97 Squadron

F/S CE Saunders
RF460/H
97 Squadron

84 Above: Washingtons of the second vic over Odiham at 1,600 feet. WF552 of 115 Squadron is the nearest, WF560 in front. The picture was probably taken from S/L O'N Fisher's machine, WF566, of 207 Squadron

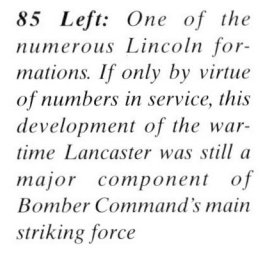

85 Left: One of the numerous Lincoln formations. If only by virtue of numbers in service, this development of the wartime Lancaster was still a major component of Bomber Command's main striking force

86: A first cousin to the Lancaster, Shackletons of Coastal Command drone overhead. At the time, few would have guessed that the type still had over thirty years of service ahead of it

© M.D.Howley 1998

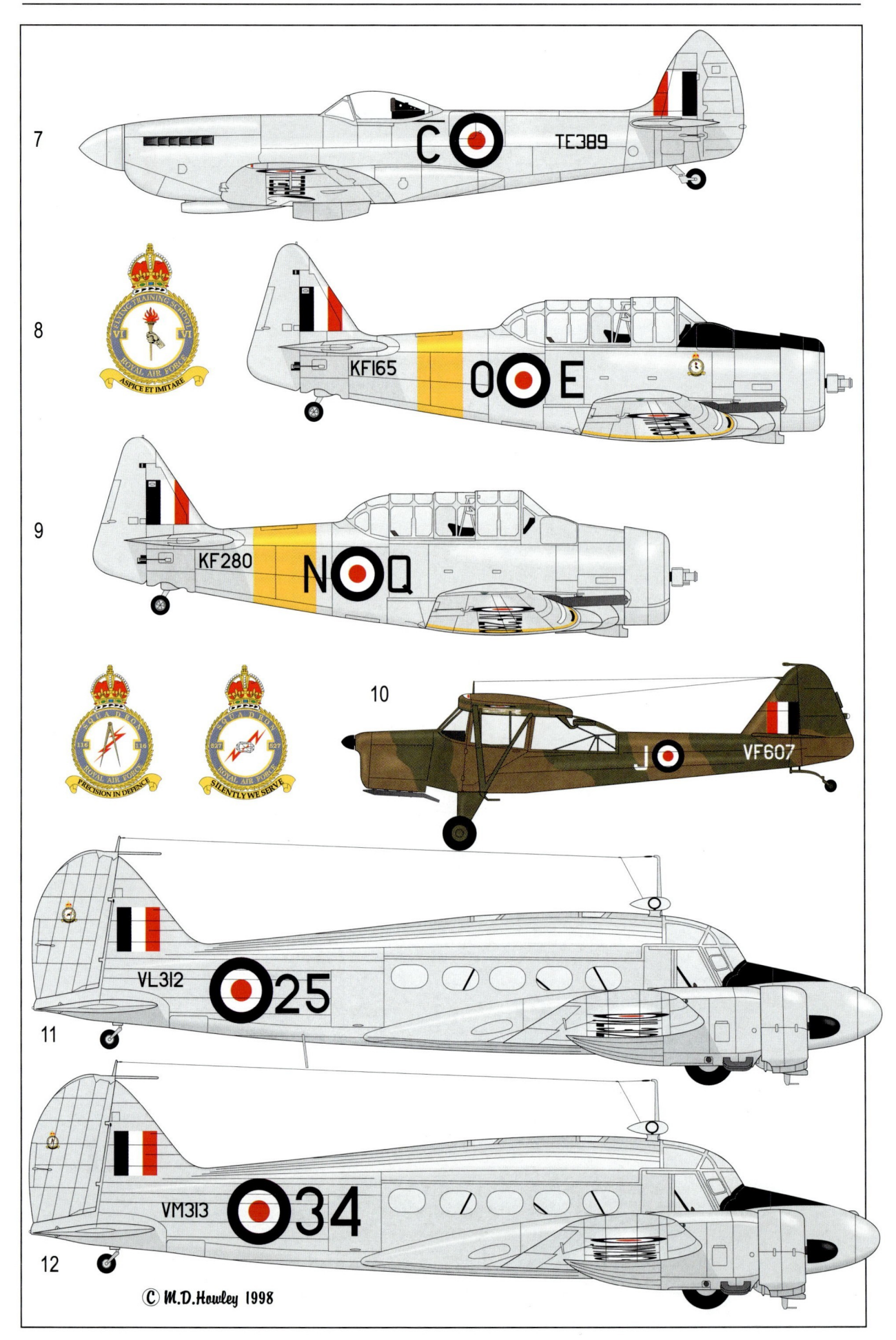

49

13 VP966

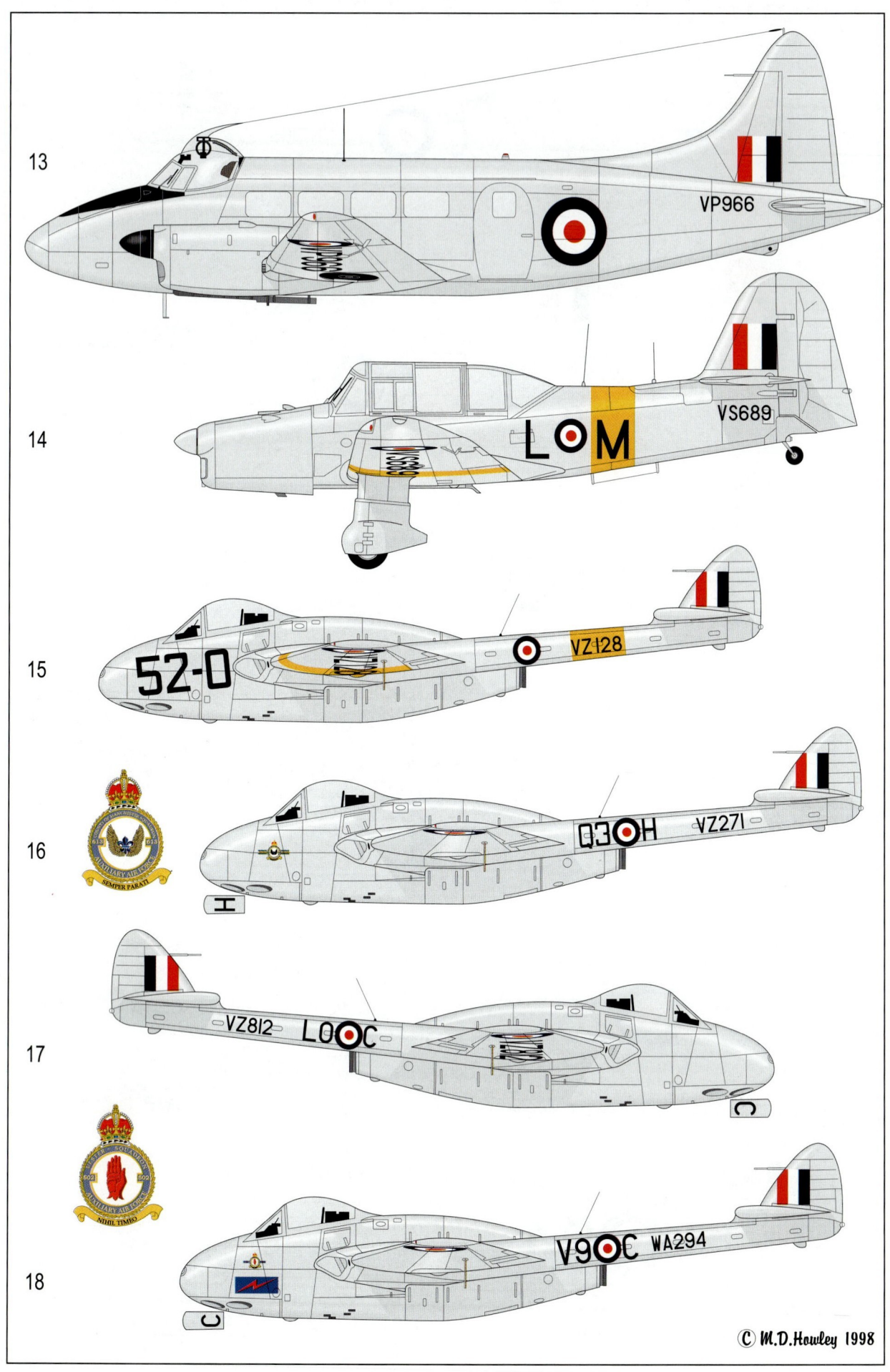

14 VS689 L·M

15 52-O VZ128

16 Q3·H VZ271

17 VZ812 L·C

18 V9·C WA294

© M.D.Howley 1998

51

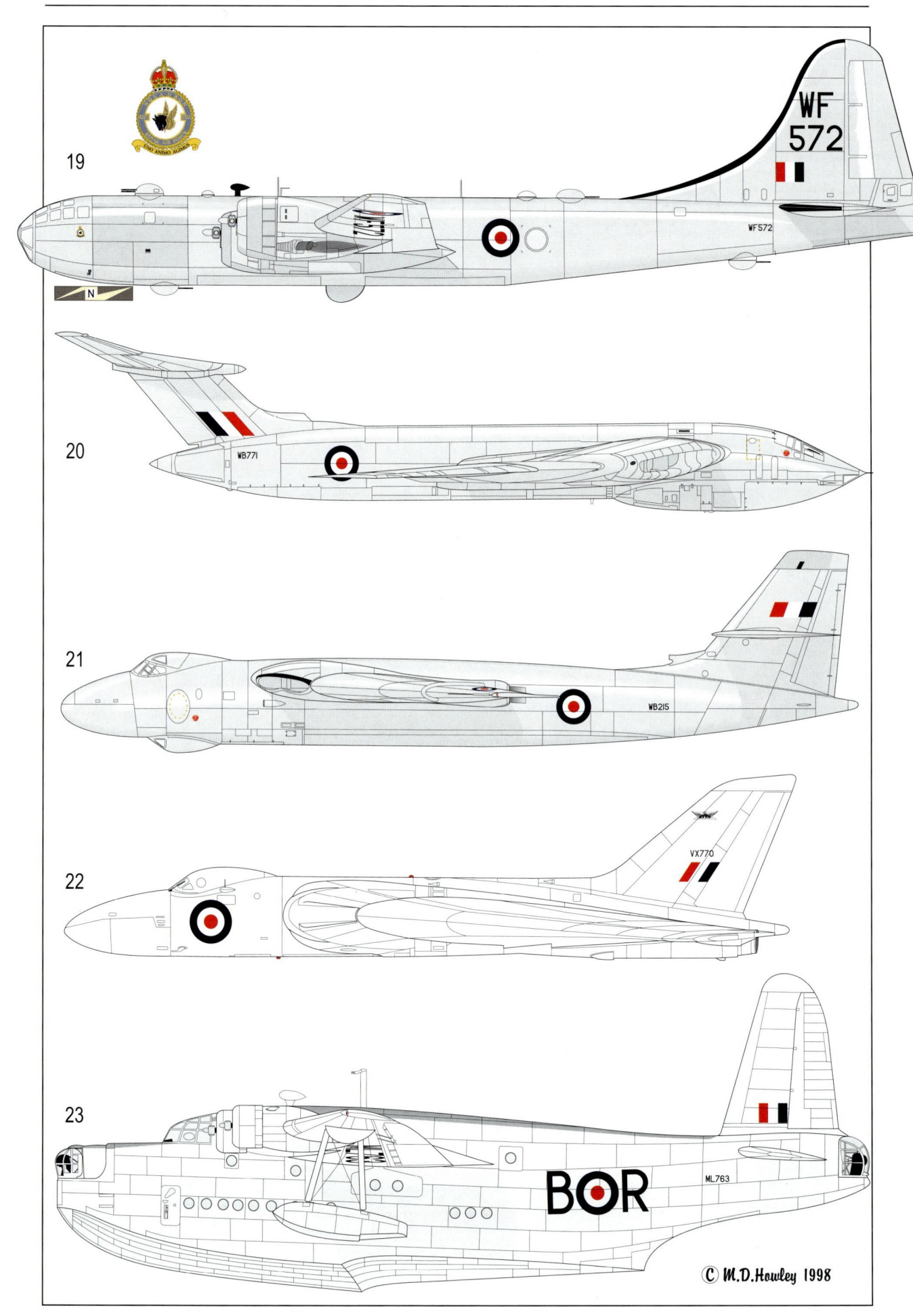

24
25
26
27
28
29

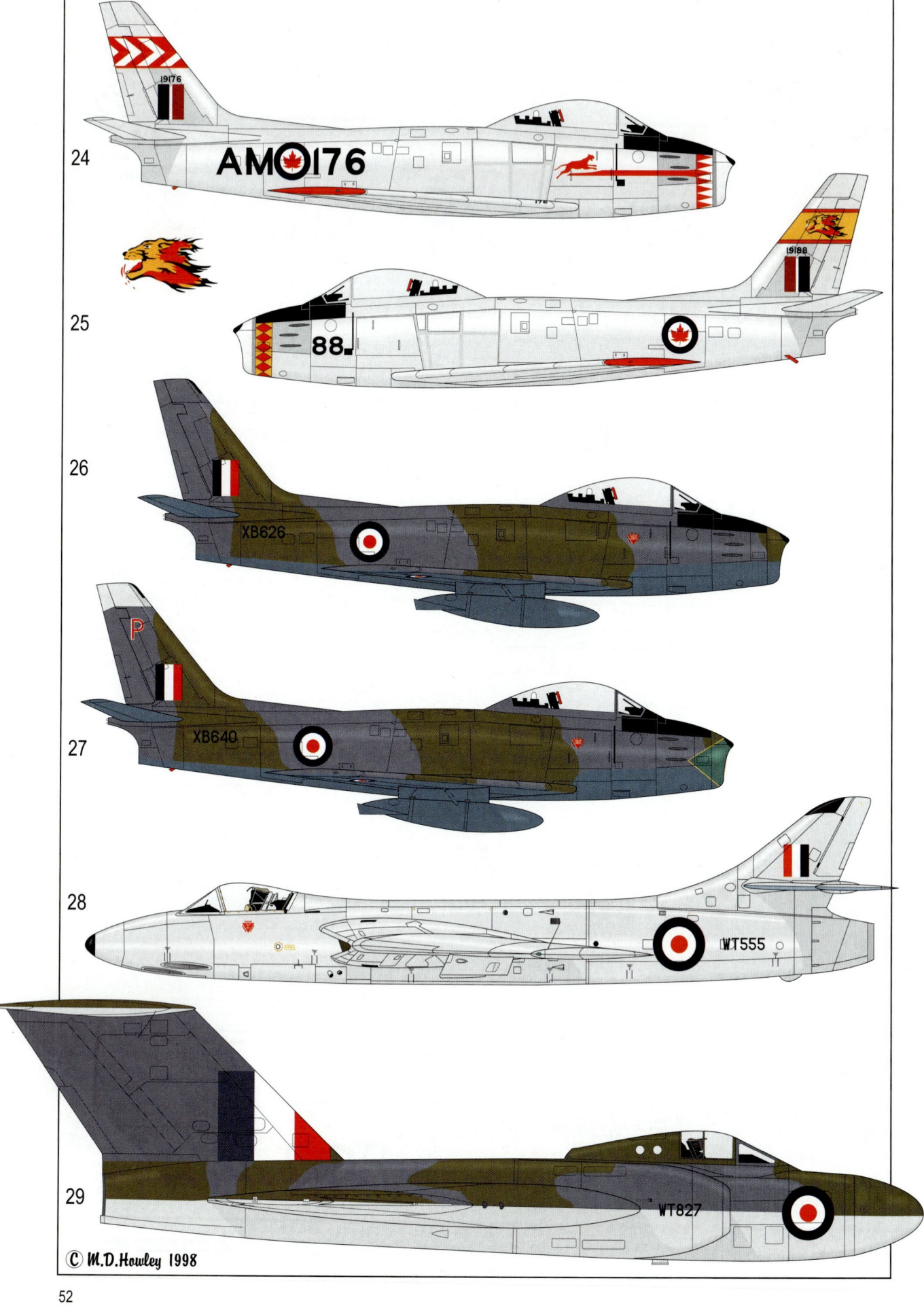

© M.D.Howley 1998

52

30 EE359

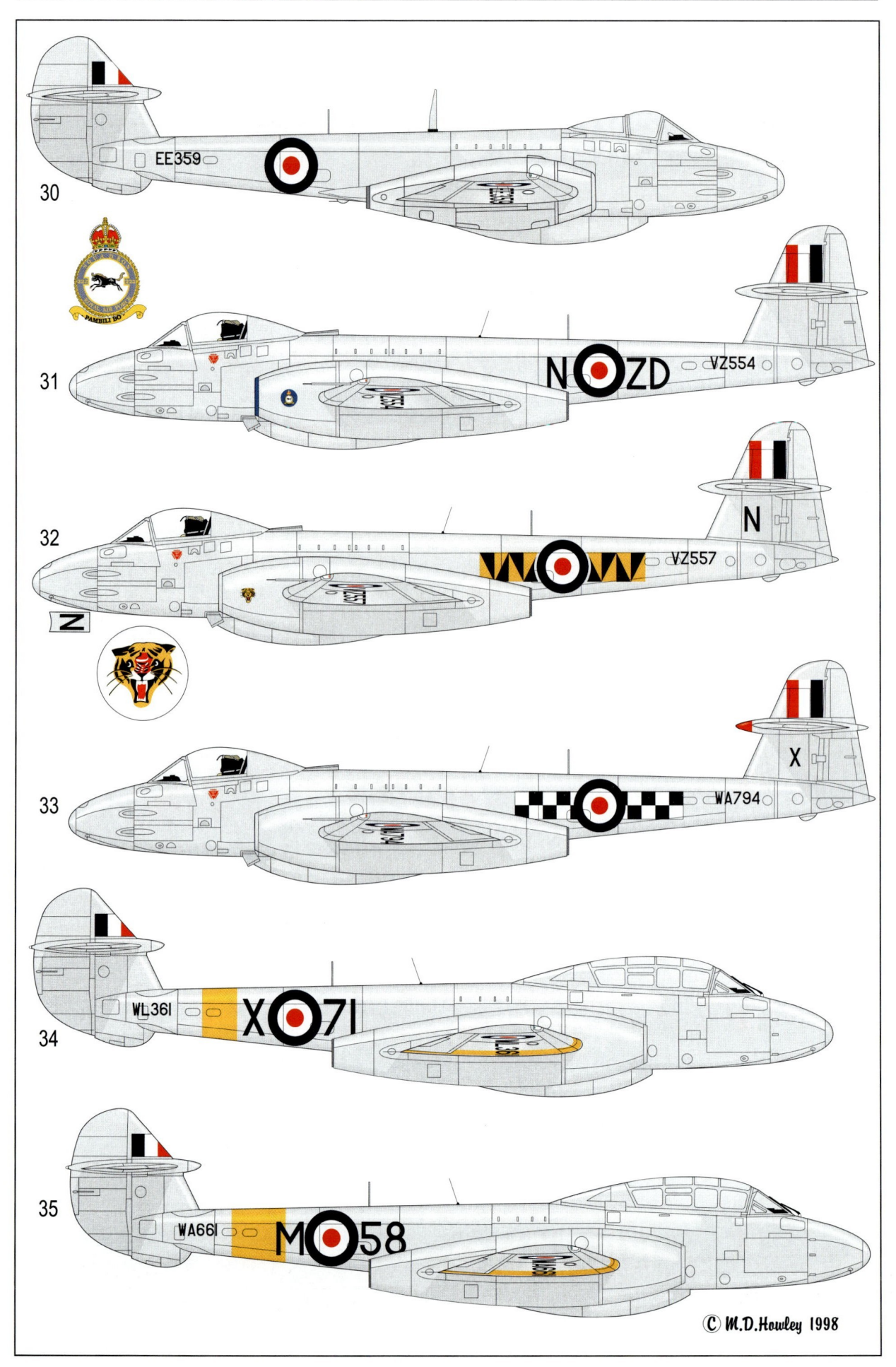

31 VZ554 N ZD

32 VZ557 N

33 WA794 X

34 WL361 X 71

35 WA661 M 58

© M.D.Howley 1998

53

36 SX926

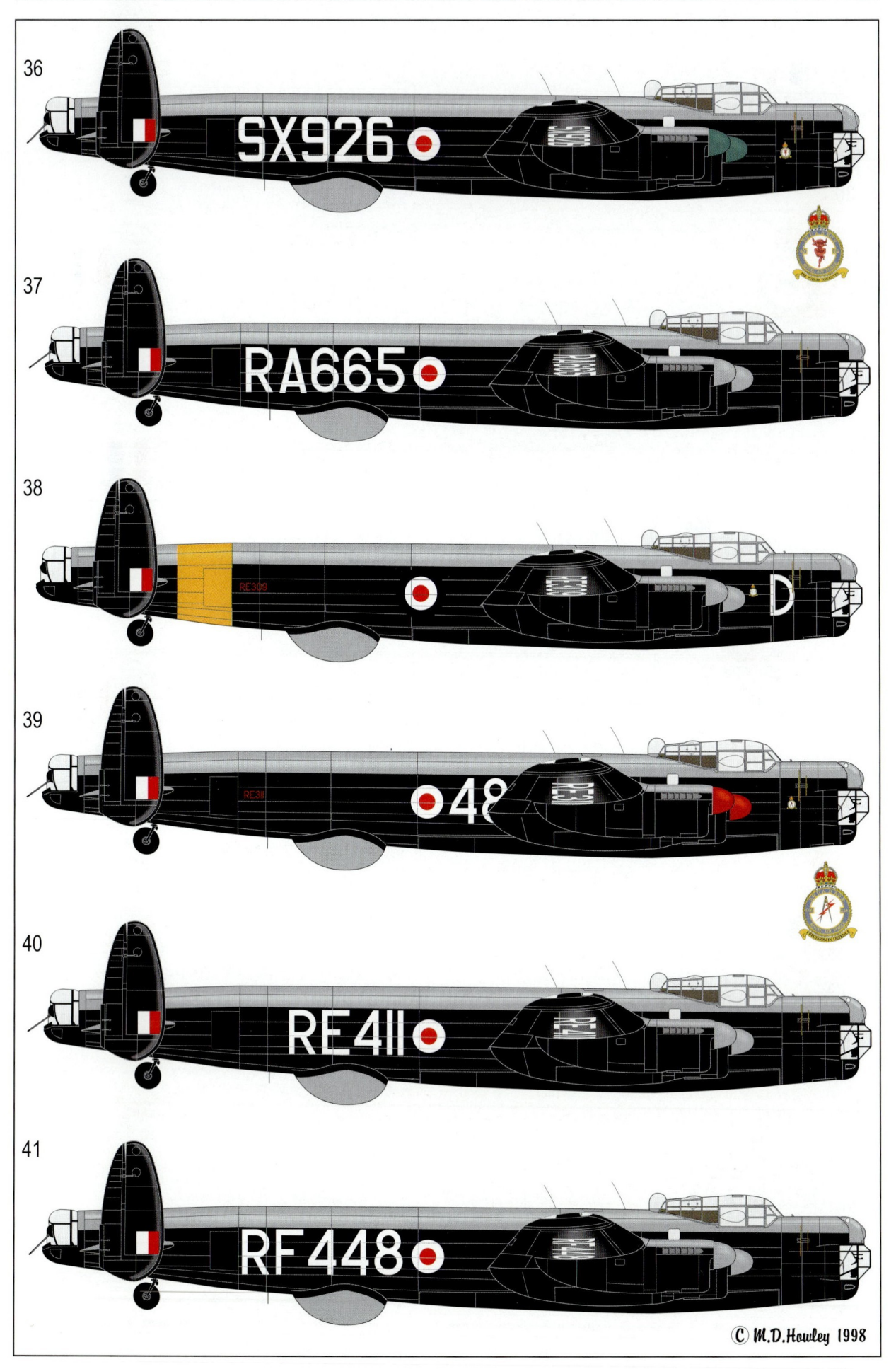

37 RA665

38 RE309 D

39 48

40 RE411

41 RF448

© M.D.Howley 1998

42

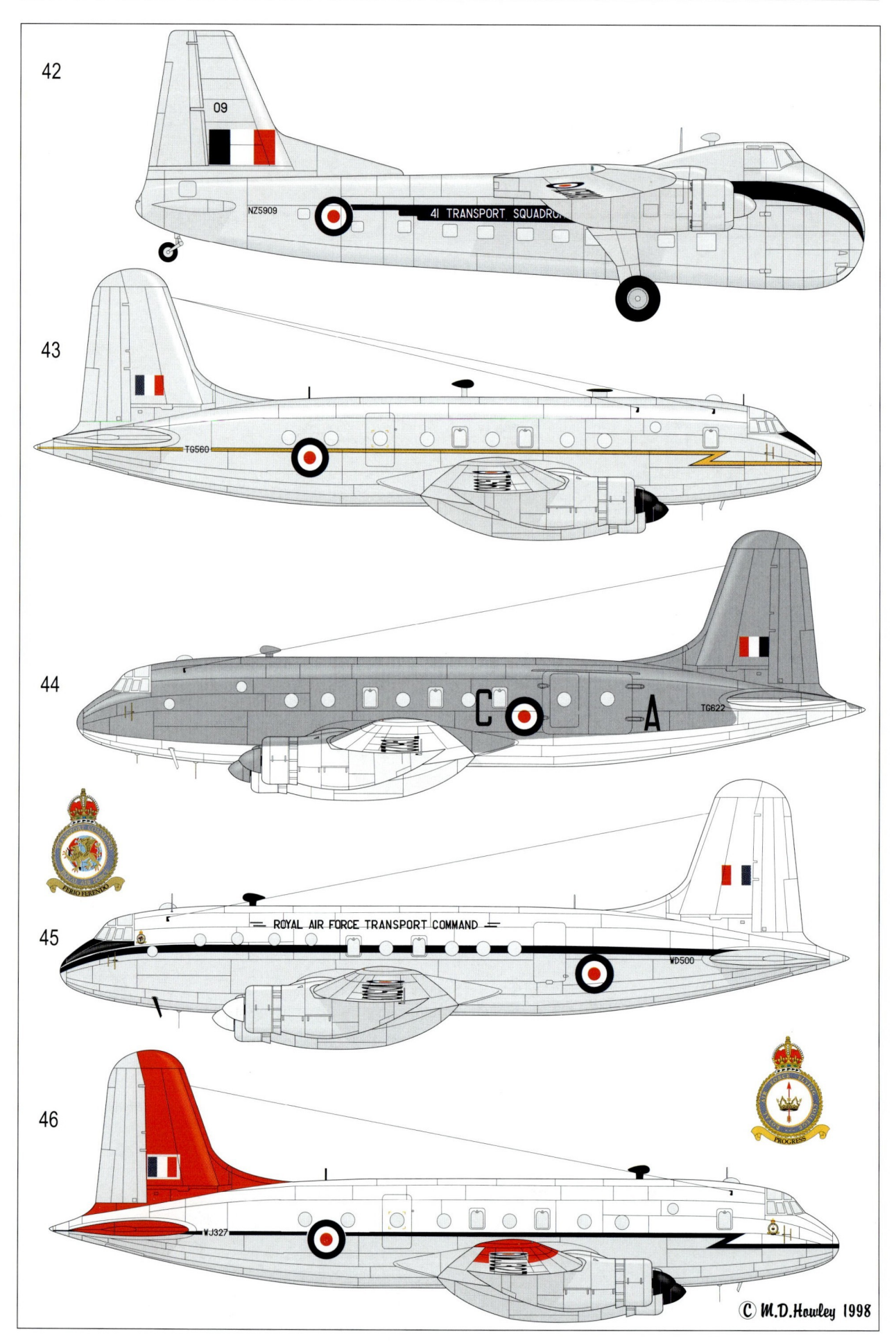

43

44

45

46

© M.D.Howley 1998

55

47

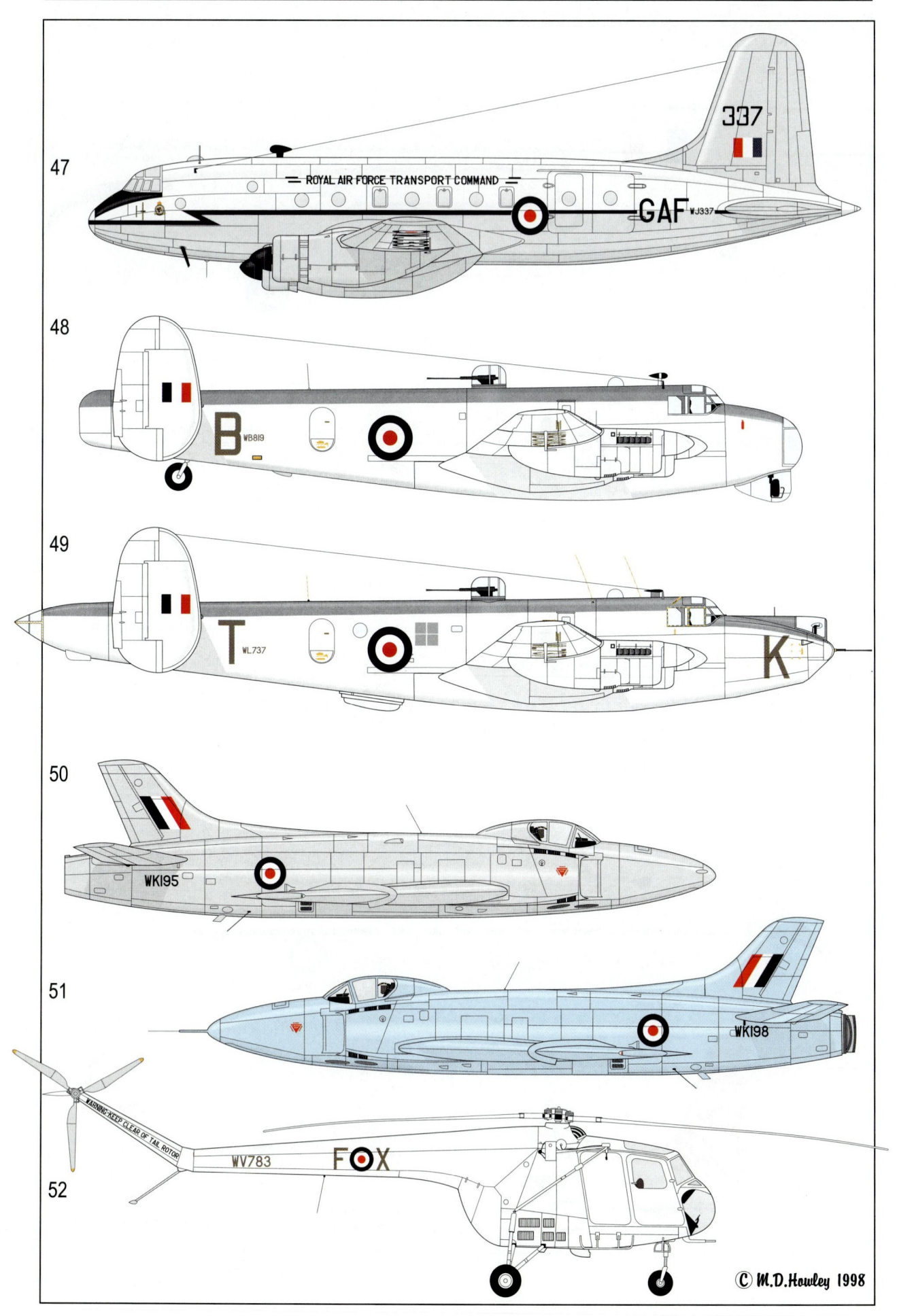

48

49

50

51

52

© M.D.Howley 1998

53

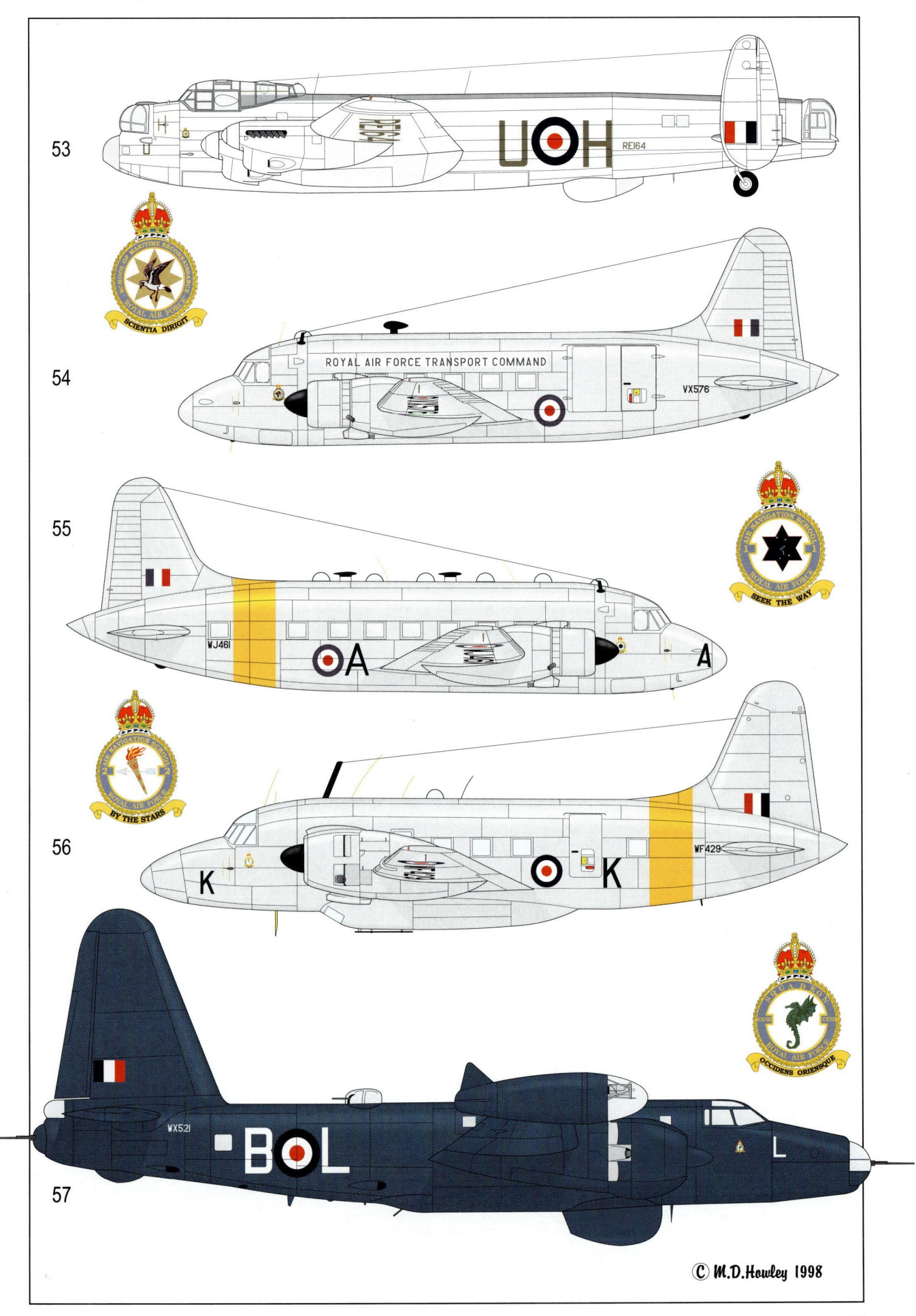

54

55

56

57

© M.D.Howley 1998

57

58 WX213

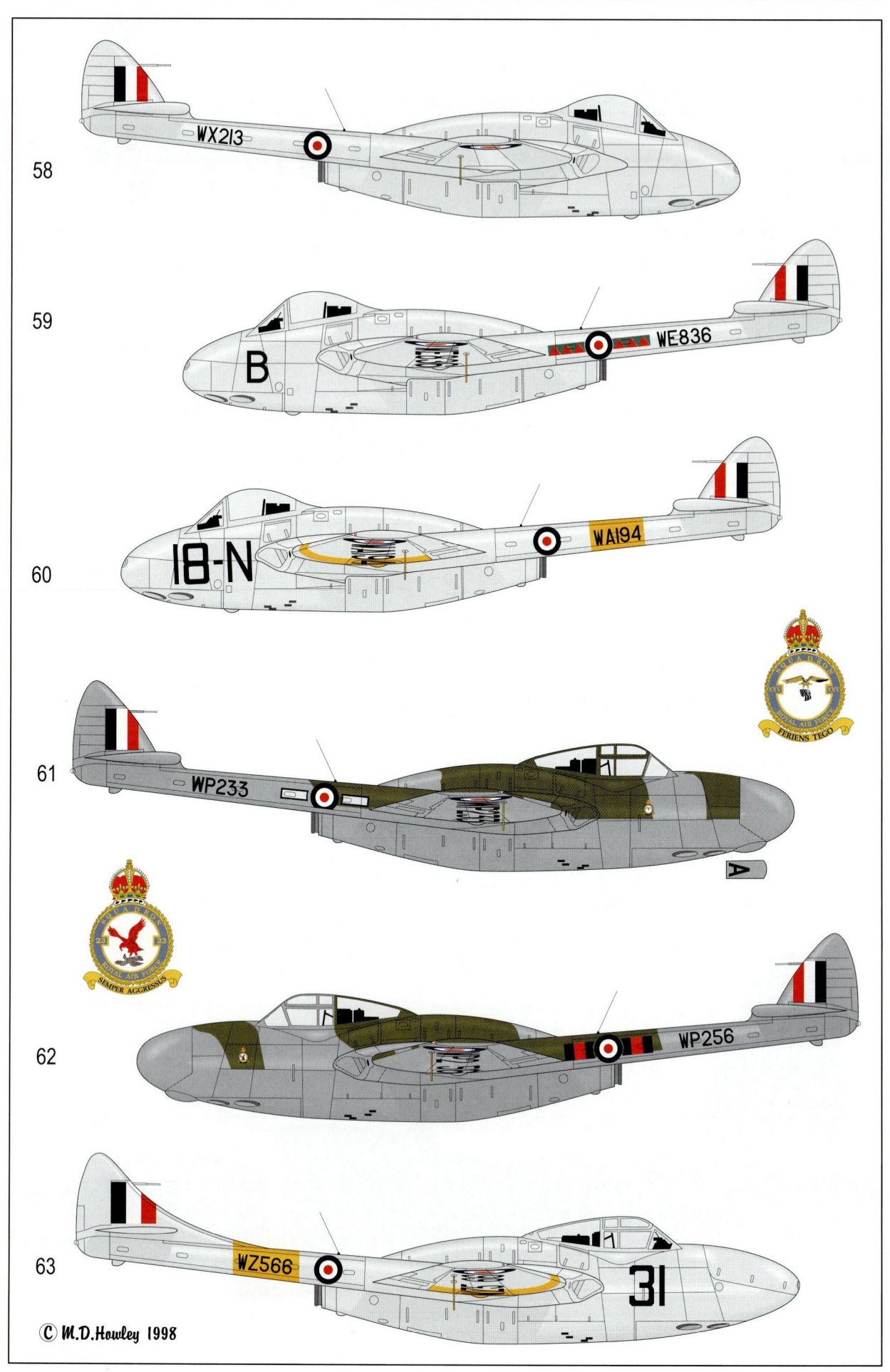

59 B WE836

60 18-N WA194

61 WP233

62 WP256

63 WZ566 31

© M.D.Howley 1998

64

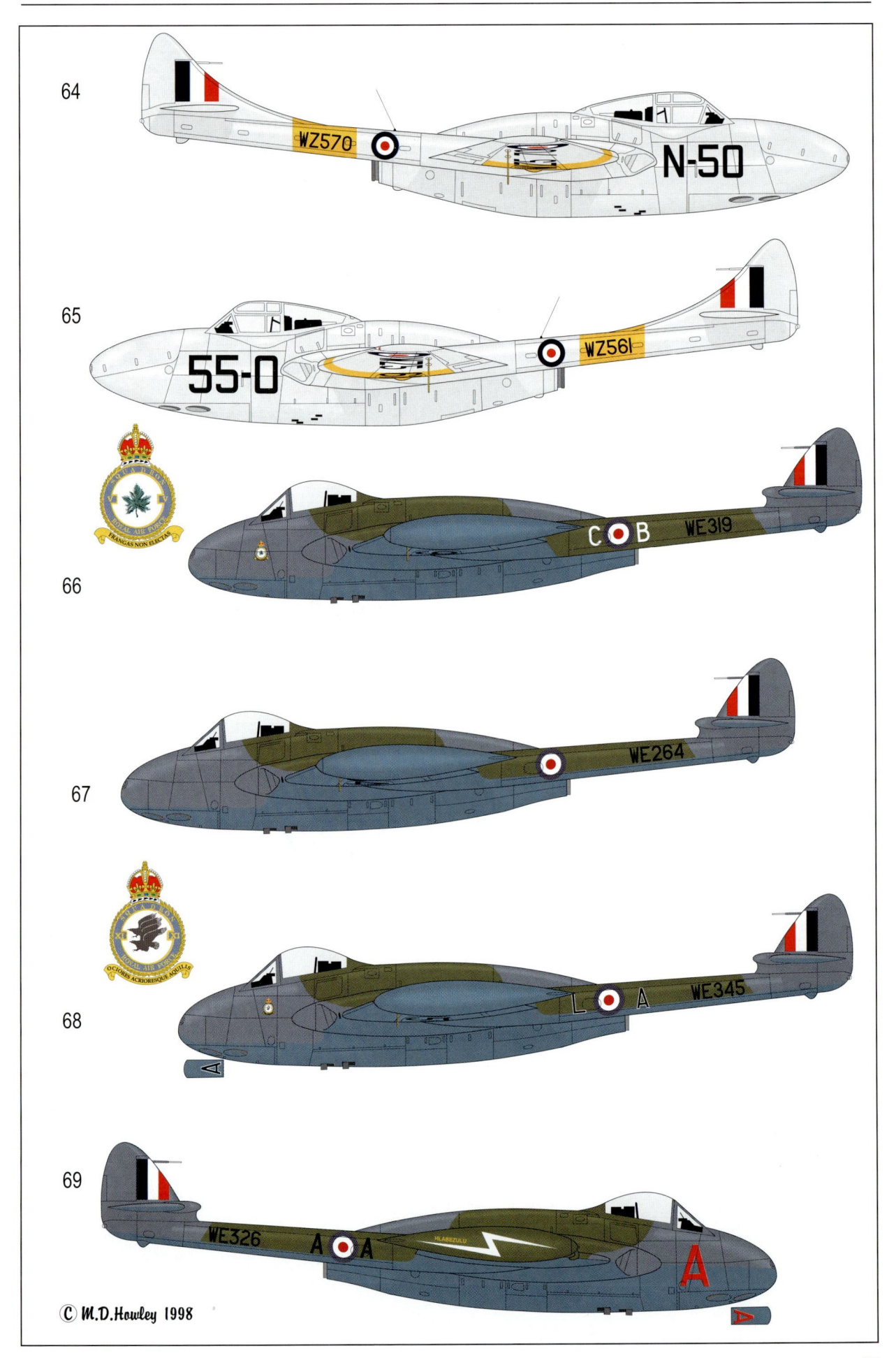

65

66

67

68

69

© M.D.Howley 1998

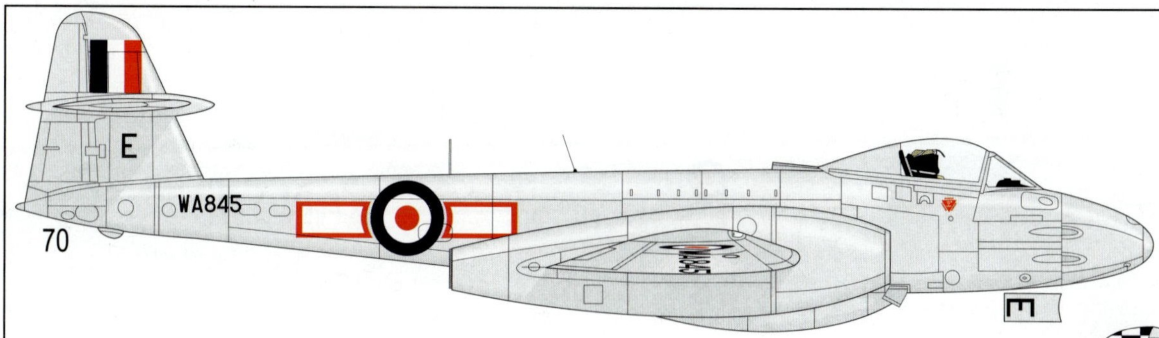

70

71

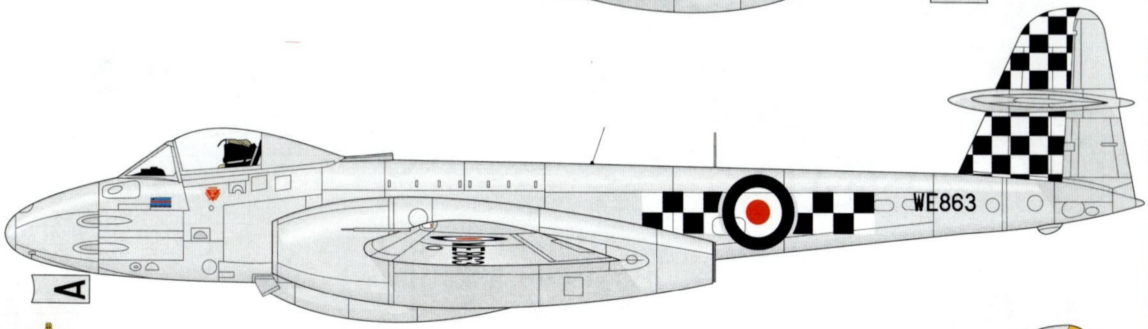

72

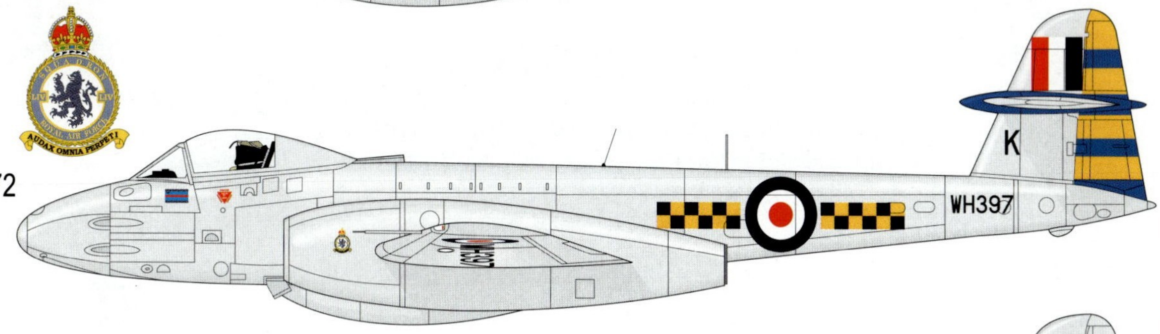

73

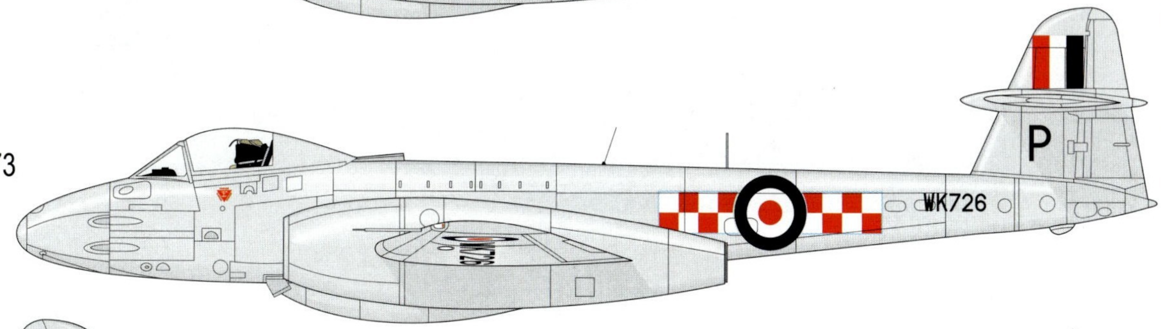

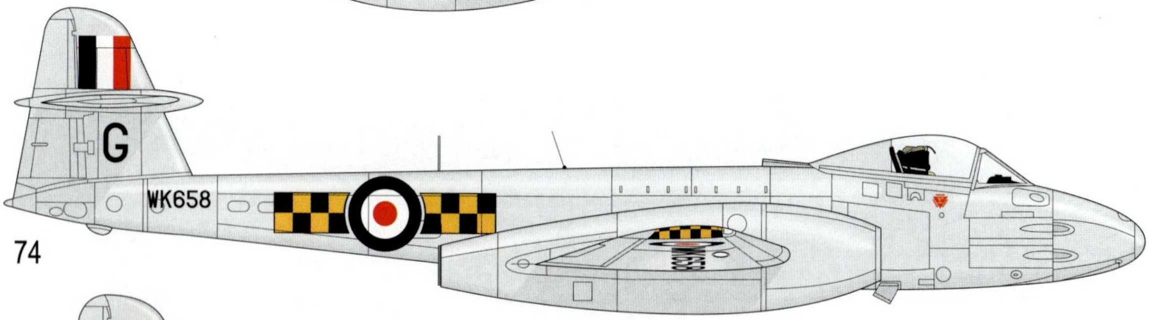

74

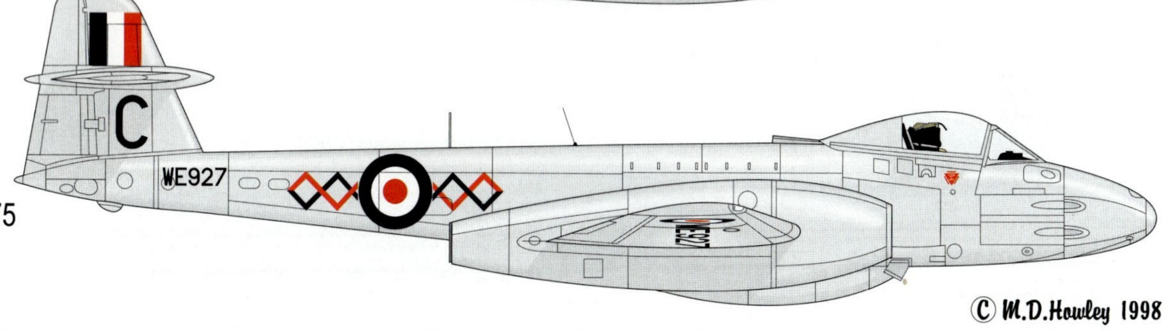

75

76

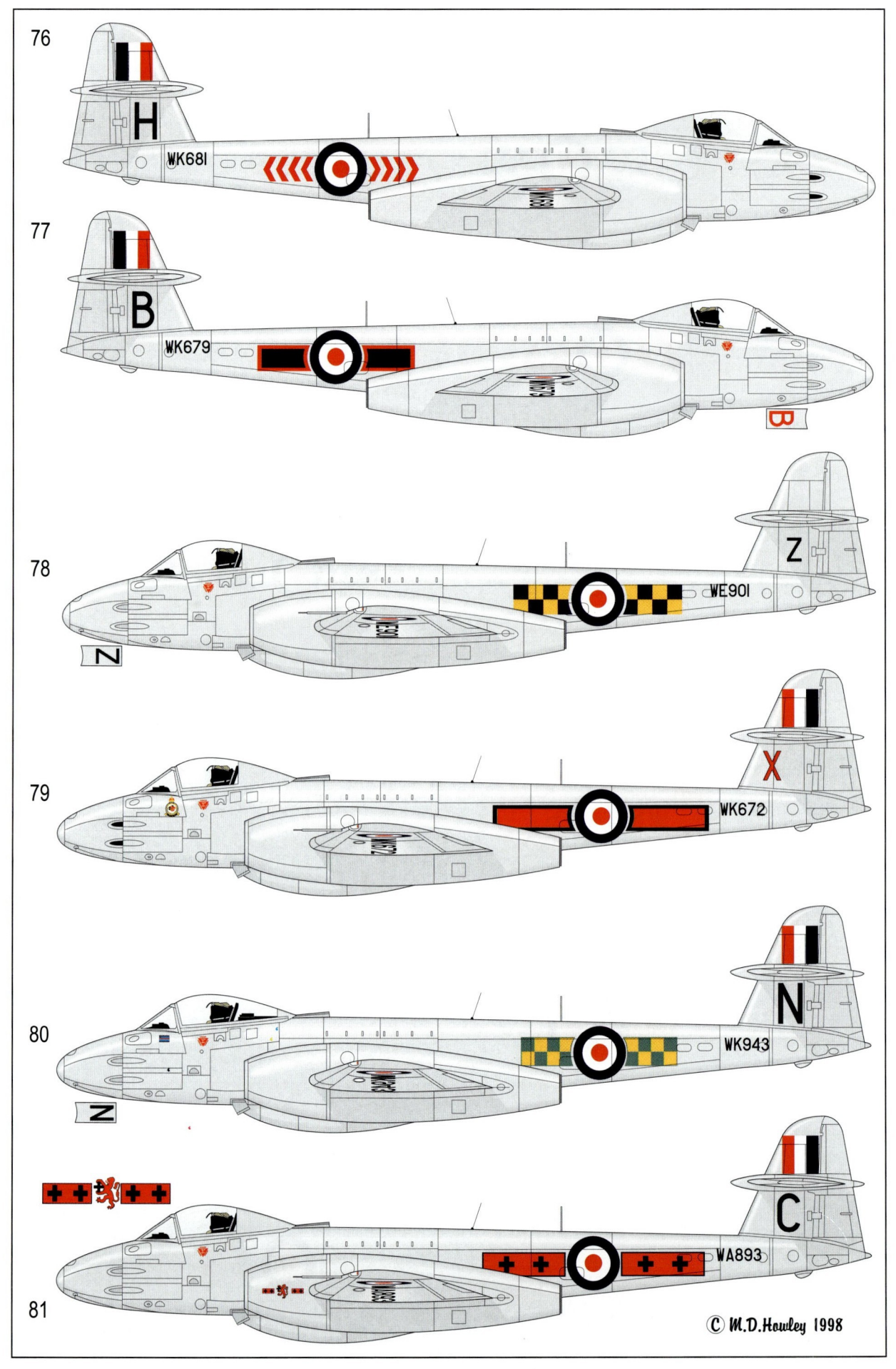

77

78

79

80

81

© M.D.Howley 1998

61

82 WH451 G

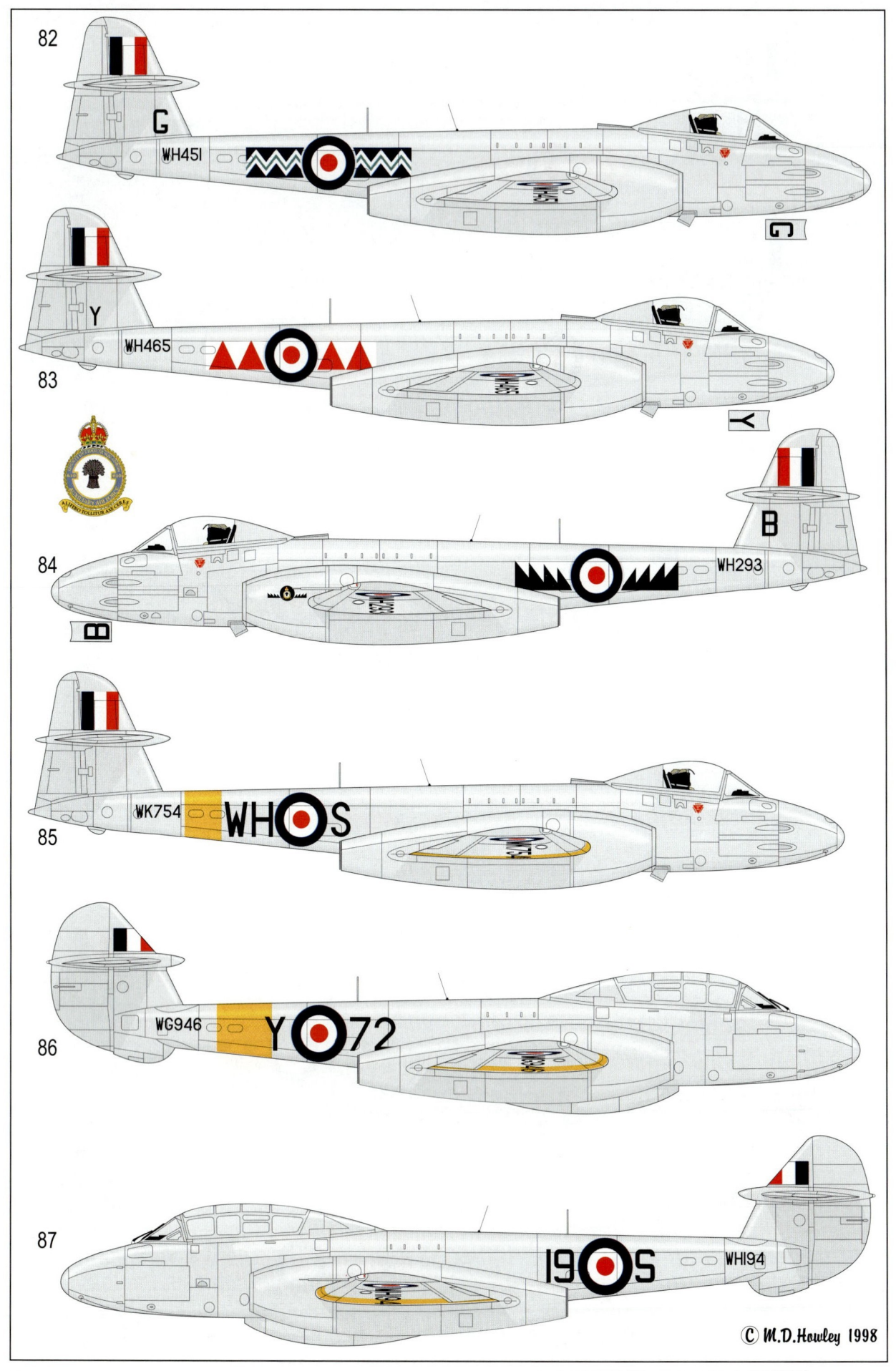

83 WH465 Y

84 WH293 B

85 WK754 WH S

86 WG946 Y 72

87 WH194 19 S

© M.D.Howley 1998

© M.D.Howley 1998

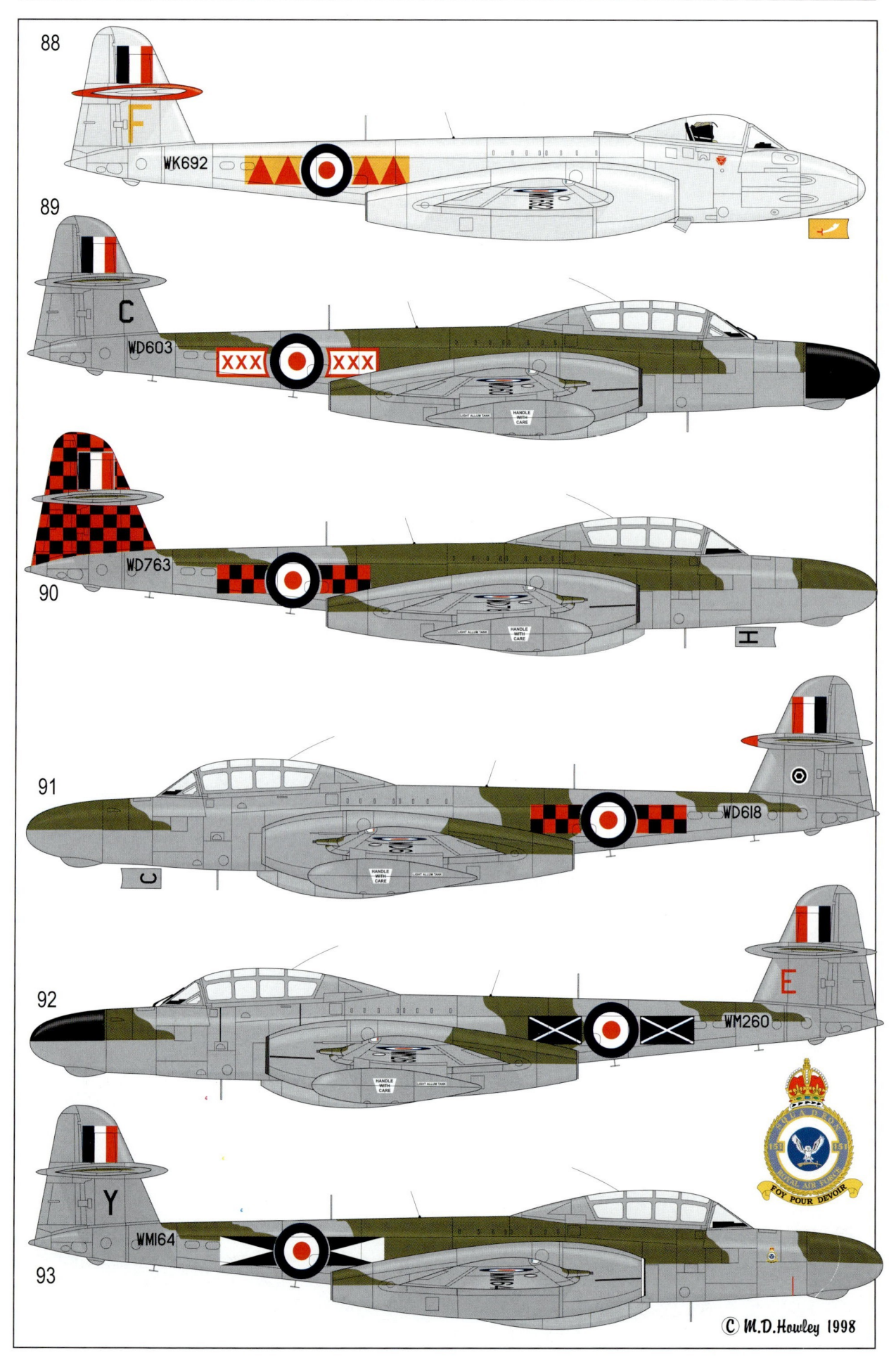

63

94

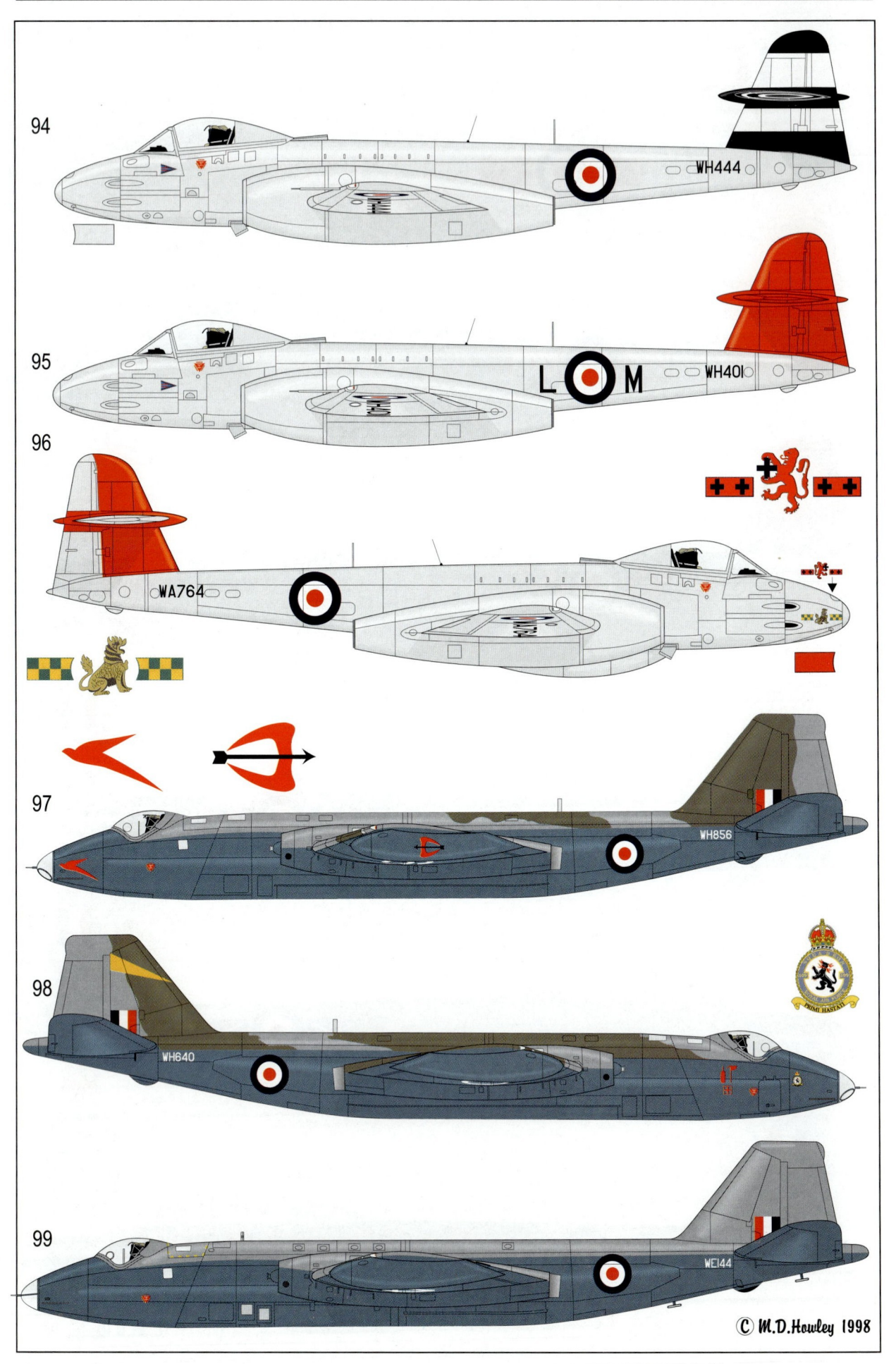

95

96

97

98

99

WH444

WH401

WA764

WH856

WH640

WE144

© M.D.Howley 1998

W/C HNG Wheeler
WW351
35 Squadron

F/L RA Patterson
WW348
35 Squadron

S/L FR Flynn
WW344
35 Squadron

S/L LG Holmes
WF560
115 Squadron

S/L RG Wilson
WF563
90 Squadron

F/L JB Cowton
WF513
115 Squadron

F/O KM Williamson
WF552
115 Squadron

F/L FN Ramsey
WF558
90 Squadron

F/O RW Stafford
WF550
90 Squadron

S/L GW O'N Fisher
WF566
207 Squadron

F/L EM Stewart
WF569
207 Squadron

F/L CJ Petheram
WF567
207 Squadron

FORMATION 18

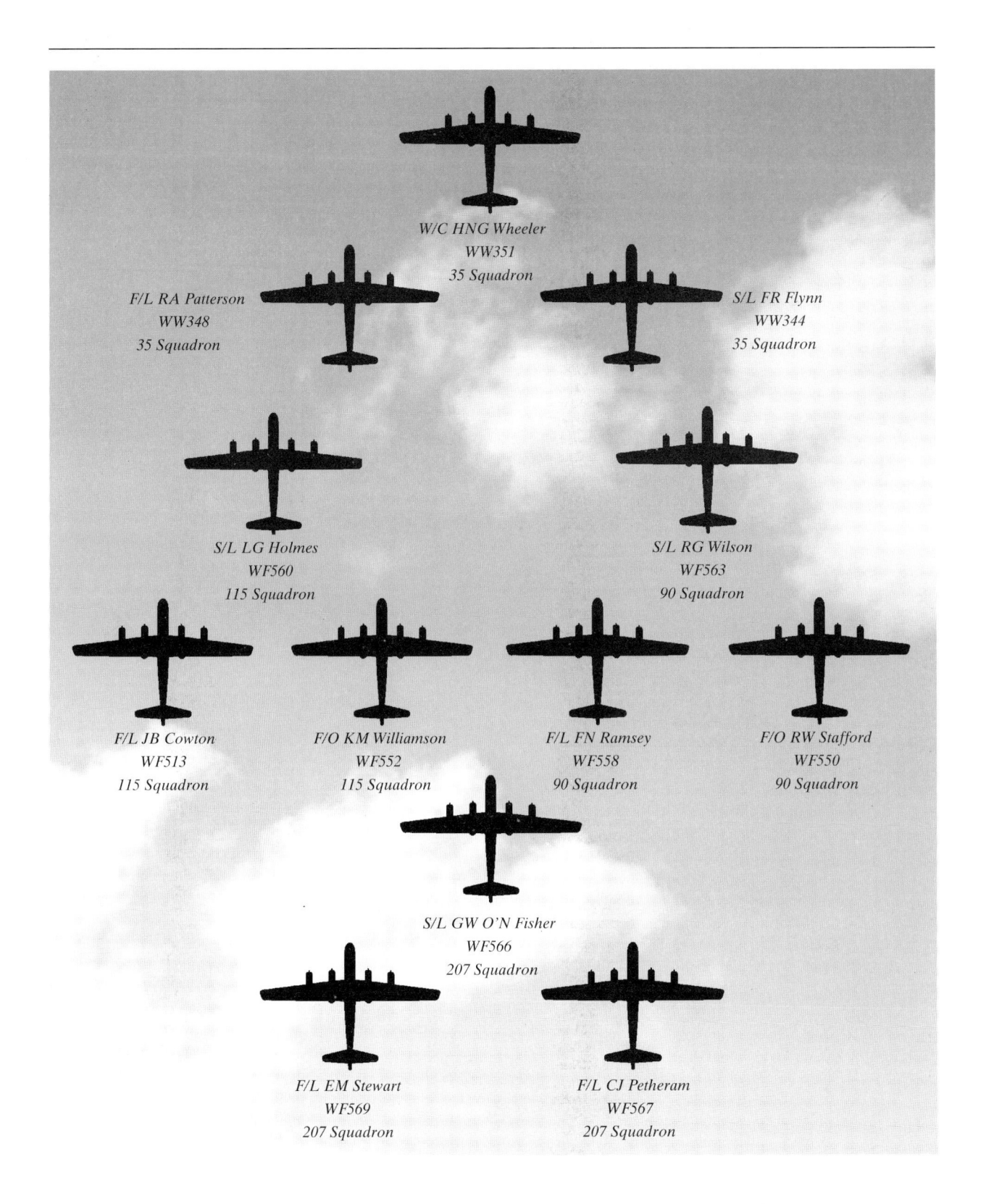

Bomber Command

12 Boeing Washington B.1s from 35, 115 and 207 Squadrons, operated from Marham

Time over Odiham: 15.49:50

Altitude: 1,600 feet

Speed: 195 mph/170 knots

Notes: *Serials all come from the Form 541 record*

Serials for 115 Squadron aircraft are confirmed by photos taken on 15 July

WW348 is confirmed from the pilot's logbook

FORMATION 19

Coastal Command
9 Avro Shackleton MR.1 and MR.2s from 42, 206 and 220 Squadrons, operated from St. Eval

Time over Odiham: 15.50·25
Altitude: 1,100 feet
Speed: 195 mph/170 knots

Notes: *Serials all come from the Form 541 record. Codes are confirmed by photos taken on 15 July*

S/L AEW Laband
WL745/T-O
220 Squadron

F/L HHJ Browning
WL737/T-K
220 Squadron

F/O M Earle
WL743/T-P
220 Squadron

F/L RH Stubbs
WG556/A-J
42 Squadron

F/L RCB Ashworth
WG525
42 Squadron

F/L CFP Thompson
WG526/A-C
42 Squadron

F/L CH Biddie
WG558
206 Squadron

F/O NG Allsop
WG528/A-B
206 Squadron

Lt Legg
WG508/L-F
206 Squadron

66

FORMATION 20

Coastal Command
9 Avro Shackleton MR.1 and MR.2s from 120, 240 and 269 Squadrons, operated from Ballykelly

Time over Odiham: 15.51
Altitude: 1,600 feet
Speed: 195 mph/170 knots

Notes: Serials all come from the Form 541 record and are confirmed by photos taken on 15 July

WL748 is confirmed from a photo taken on 15 July, although F/L Hurrell's logbook and the Form 541 both record WL738

WL750 and WG507 are confirmed from pilots' logbooks

WG507 seems to have been borrowed from 240 Squadron for the 269 Squadron formation

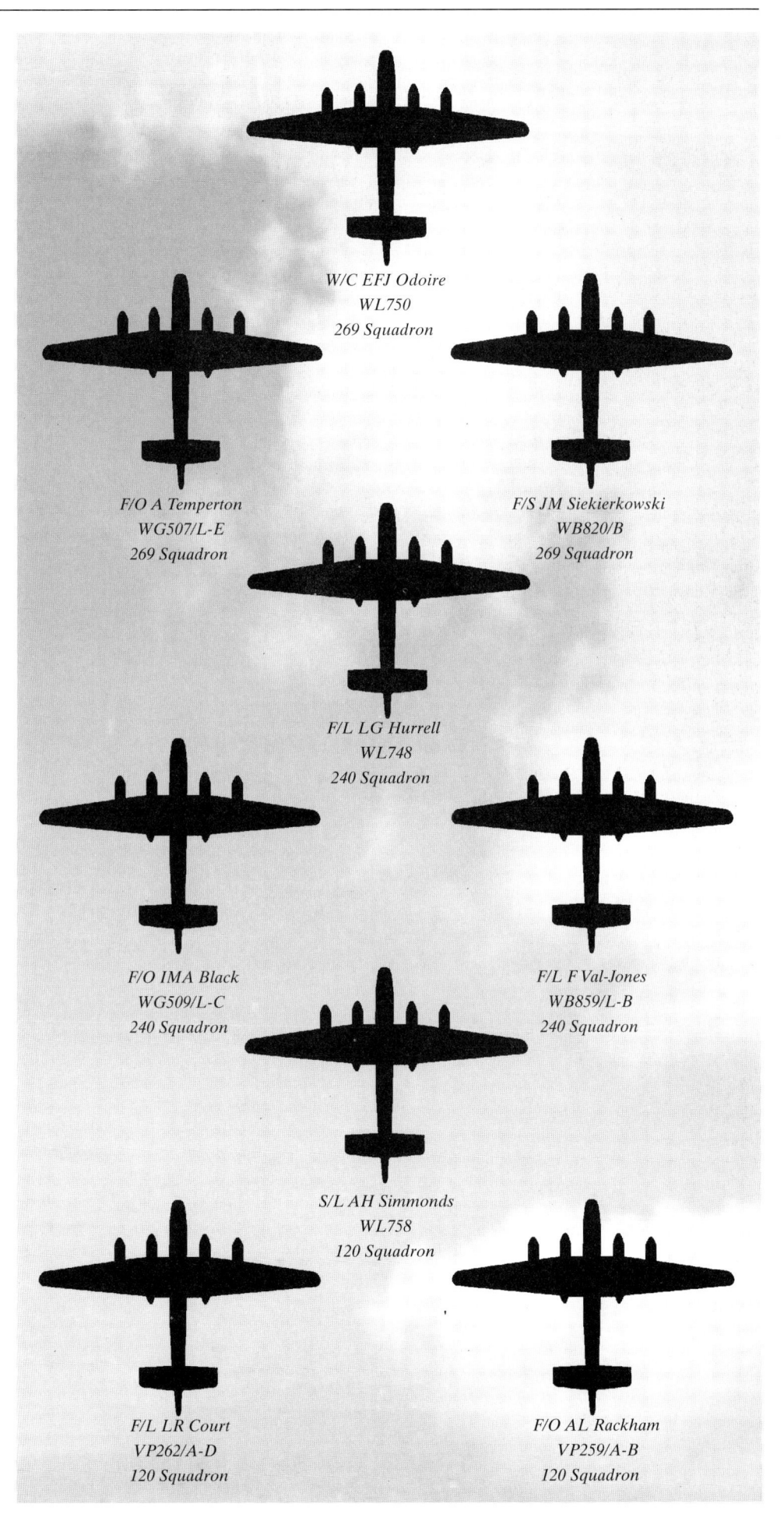

W/C EFJ Odoire
WL750
269 Squadron

F/O A Temperton
WG507/L-E
269 Squadron

F/S JM Siekierkowski
WB820/B
269 Squadron

F/L LG Hurrell
WL748
240 Squadron

F/O IMA Black
WG509/L-C
240 Squadron

F/L F Val-Jones
WB859/L-B
240 Squadron

S/L AH Simmonds
WL758
120 Squadron

F/L LR Court
VP262/A-D
120 Squadron

F/O AL Rackham
VP259/A-B
120 Squadron

67

S/L MA Ensor
WX554/A-A

F/O Carpenter
WX504/A-H

F/L Stewart
WX528/L-Y

F/L Dawes
WX516/L-T

F/L EE Stocker
WX512/A-B

FORMATION 21

Coastal Command

5 Lockheed Neptune MR.1s from 217 Squadron, operated from Kinloss

Time over Odiham: 15.51 75
Altitude: 1,100 feet
Speed: 195 mph/170 knots

Notes: Although WX516 and WX528 carried 210 Squadron codes, the Operational record Book implies that the pilots were all from 217 Squadron. Serials all come from the Form 541 record

The codes are confirmed by a photo taken on 15 July

FORMATION 22

Transport/Maintenance Command

3 Handley Page Hasting C.2s from 47 and 511 Squadrons, operated from Lyneham

Time over Odiham: 15.52 50
Altitude: 1,600 feet
Speed: 195 mph/170 knots

Note: Enthusiasts' records all agree that these aircraft were WD481 and WD486/Y of 47 Squadron; and WJ331/GAX of 511 Squadron

Maj JN Robb
?????

F/L NG Emslie
?????

F/L AA Fenn
?????

FORMATION 23

Fighter Command

12 De Havilland Vampire NF.10s from 23 and 25 Squadrons, operated from Coltishall

Time over Odiham: 15.53 50
Altitude: 1,100 feet
Speed: 305 mph/265 knots

Note: *The formation was led by W/C JW Allan in WM705 23 Squadron; F/L JH Hedger (Leader, right box, marked with a cross in this picture taken on another occasion) in WM704 23 Squadron; F/L R Bowie, WM672 25 Squadron; F/O TS Johnson, ?/A 25 Squadron; P/O IAG Svensson, ?/B 25 Squadron and F/S Z Zmitrowicz, ?/O 25 Squadron*

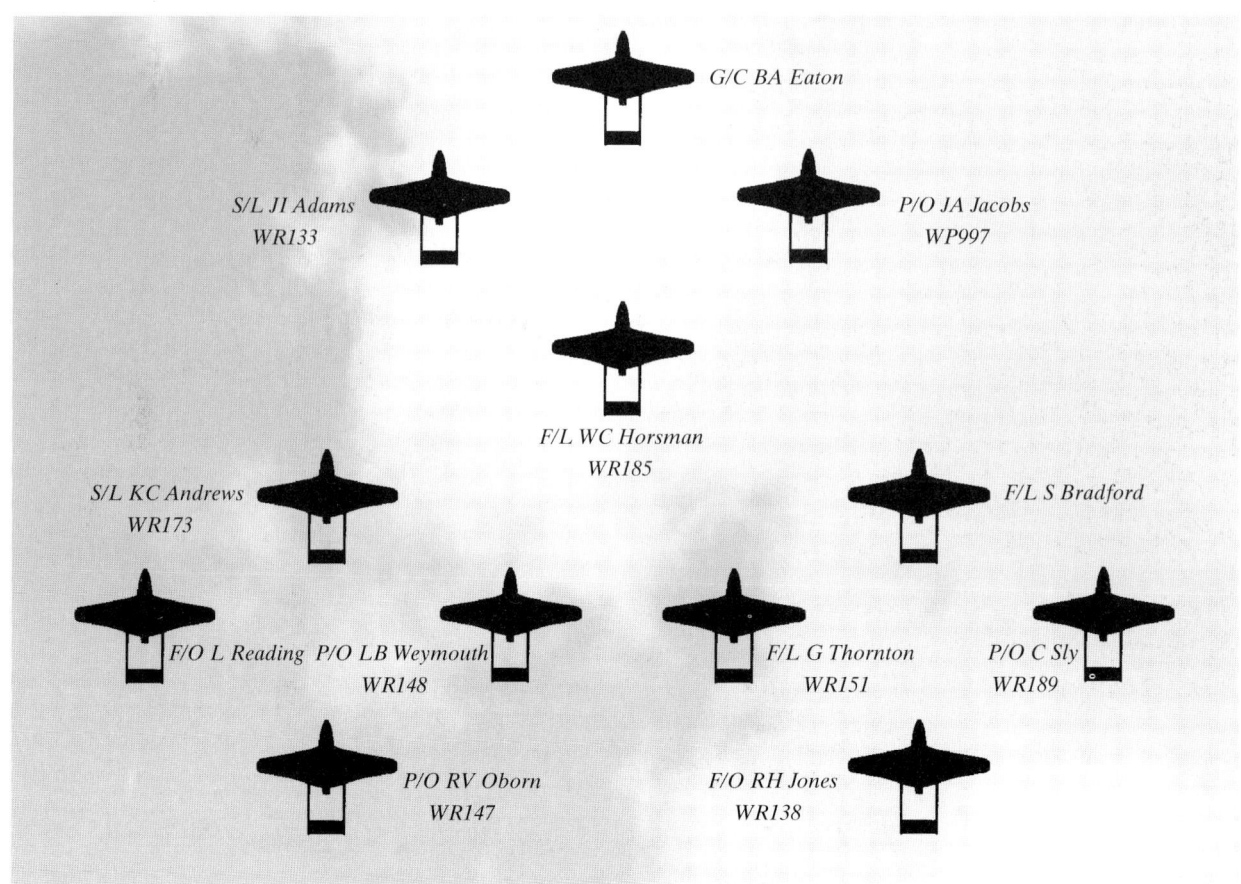

G/C BA Eaton

S/L JI Adams WR133

P/O JA Jacobs WP997

F/L WC Horsman WR185

S/L KC Andrews WR173

F/L S Bradford

F/O L Reading P/O LB Weymouth WR148

F/L G Thornton WR151

P/O C Sly WR189

P/O RV Oborn WR147

F/O RH Jones WR138

FORMATION 24

Royal Australian Air Force

12 De Havilland Vampire FB.9s from 78 Wing, RAAF Malta, operated from Horsham St. Faith

Time over Odiham: 15.54
Altitude: 1,600 feet
Speed: 305 mph/265 knots

Notes: *The Wing was composed of 75 and 76 Squadrons, RAAF, but which aircraft belonged to which squadron is not known*

G/C Eaton probably flew WR239. Listed in the record cards as 'Malta Sector Commander'

89: *Horsham St Faith was the base used by the RAAF Vampire FB.9s during their detachment from Malta. WR189, nearest the camera, was flown by P/O C Sly on the 15 July. Korean experience was to lead to a maturing of the Australian Air Force and a move away from the close ties with the RAF. This would be most evident in the later adoption of the famous kangaroo roundel*

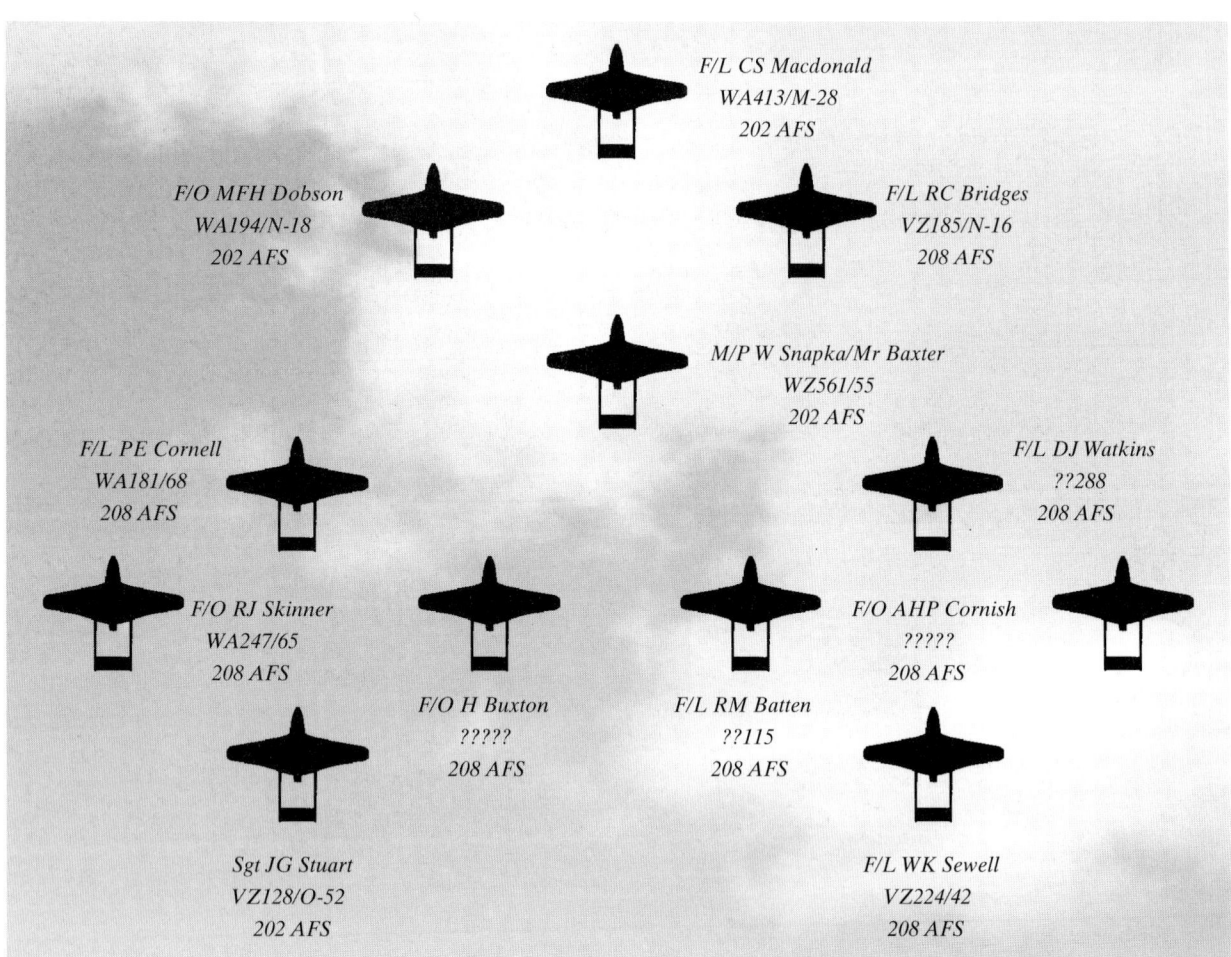

F/L CS Macdonald
WA413/M-28
202 AFS

F/O MFH Dobson
WA194/N-18
202 AFS

F/L RC Bridges
VZ185/N-16
208 AFS

M/P W Snapka/Mr Baxter
WZ561/55
202 AFS

F/L PE Cornell
WA181/68
208 AFS

F/L DJ Watkins
??288
208 AFS

F/O RJ Skinner
WA247/65
208 AFS

F/O AHP Cornish
?????
208 AFS

F/O H Buxton
?????
208 AFS

F/L RM Batten
??115
208 AFS

Sgt JG Stuart
VZ128/O-52
202 AFS

F/L WK Sewell
VZ224/42
208 AFS

FORMATION 25

Flying Training Command

11 De Havilland Vampire FB.5s and 1 De Havilland Vampire T.11 from 202 and 208 Advanced Flying Schools, operated from Oakington

Time over Odiham: 15.5450

Altitude: 1,100 feet

Speed: 305 mph/265 knots

Notes: *The serials are from pilots' logbooks. The code tie-ups are from photos taken on 11 July. The units quoted apply to both pilots and aircraft except for VZ185 which was with 202 AFS*

From the record cards, F/L Batten's aircraft could only be WA115

F/L Watkin's machine could be VZ288 or WA288, both being with 208 AFS at the time

90: *The FTC Meteors during a rehearsal on 11 July*

F/L GG Farley/M Laval
WH192/W-75
205 AFS

F/O MJS Norman
VT134
205 AFS

F/L MH Levy
RA397/O-30
203 AFS

F/L AL Hoult
?????
207 AFS

F/O MG Bradley
RA456
205 AFS

F/O TM Fennel
VT128
205 AFS

F/O D Geddes
?????
207 AFS

F/O HO Field
VZ416/O-23
203 AFS

F/O BA Ashley
RA437/S-25
207 AFS

F/O RB Morgan
VW284
203 AFS

P/O AE Pike
?????
207 AFS

F/O JP L'Estrange
VT311/O-22
203 AFS

FORMATION 26 ▲

Flying Training Command

11 Gloster Meteor F.4s and 1 Gloster Meteor T.7 from 203, 205 and 207 Advanced Flying Schools, operated from Oakington

Time over Odiham: 15.55
Altitude: 1,600 feet
Speed: 345 mph/300 knots

Notes: *The serials are from pilots' logbooks. The codes are confirmed from photos taken on 11 July. Units apply to the pilots, who flew aircraft from their own schools except for WH192 which was with 206 AFS and VW284 which was with 205 AFS*

71

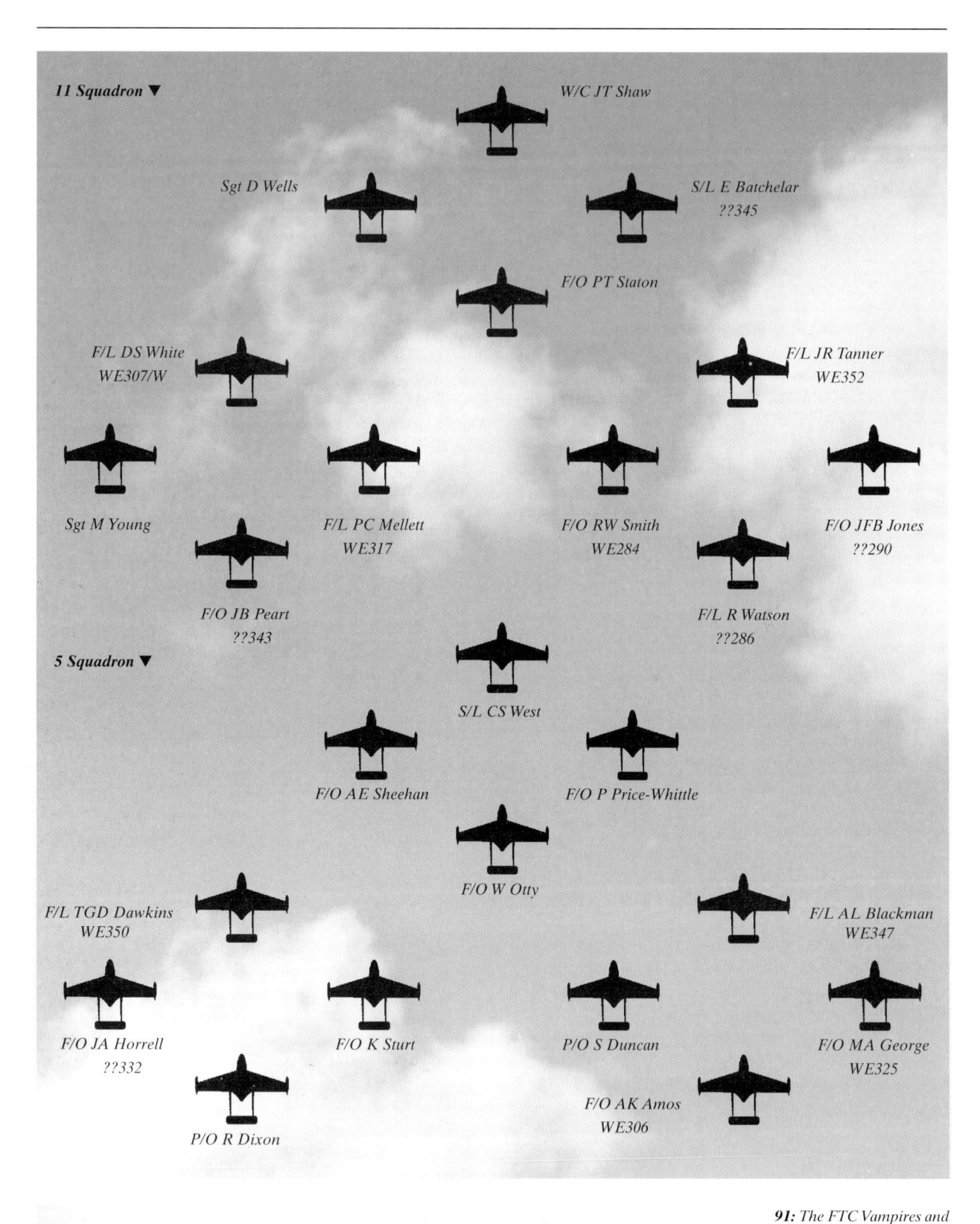

11 Squadron ▼

W/C JT Shaw

Sgt D Wells

S/L E Batchelar
??345

F/O PT Staton

F/L DS White
WE307/W

F/L JR Tanner
WE352

Sgt M Young

F/L PC Mellett
WE317

F/O RW Smith
WE284

F/O JFB Jones
??290

F/O JB Peart
??343

F/L R Watson
??286

5 Squadron ▼

S/L CS West

F/O AE Sheehan

F/O P Price-Whittle

F/O W Otty

F/L TGD Dawkins
WE350

F/L AL Blackman
WE347

F/O JA Horrell
??332

F/O K Sturt

P/O S Duncan

F/O MA George
WE325

P/O R Dixon

F/O AK Amos
WE306

91: *The FTC Vampires and Meteors on the runway at Oakington, probably during a rehearsal. There are 13 Vampires and 14 Meteors visible on the original print, but neither Vampire T.11 WZ561 or Vampire FB.5, VZ128 can be seen*

54 Squadron ▼

W/C D Crowley-Milling
??444/CM

F/O RJ Davis

F/L MH Castle

Capt HB Arnold

S/L PJ Kelley

F/L BRA Cox
WK879

F/L AR Satow
WH404

F/O DC Bingham
WK710

F/O BJ Noble
WK707

F/L MJ Bridges
?????/S

F/O PJ Thrower
WA825

??

247 Squadron ▼

S/L HG Pattison
?????/P

??

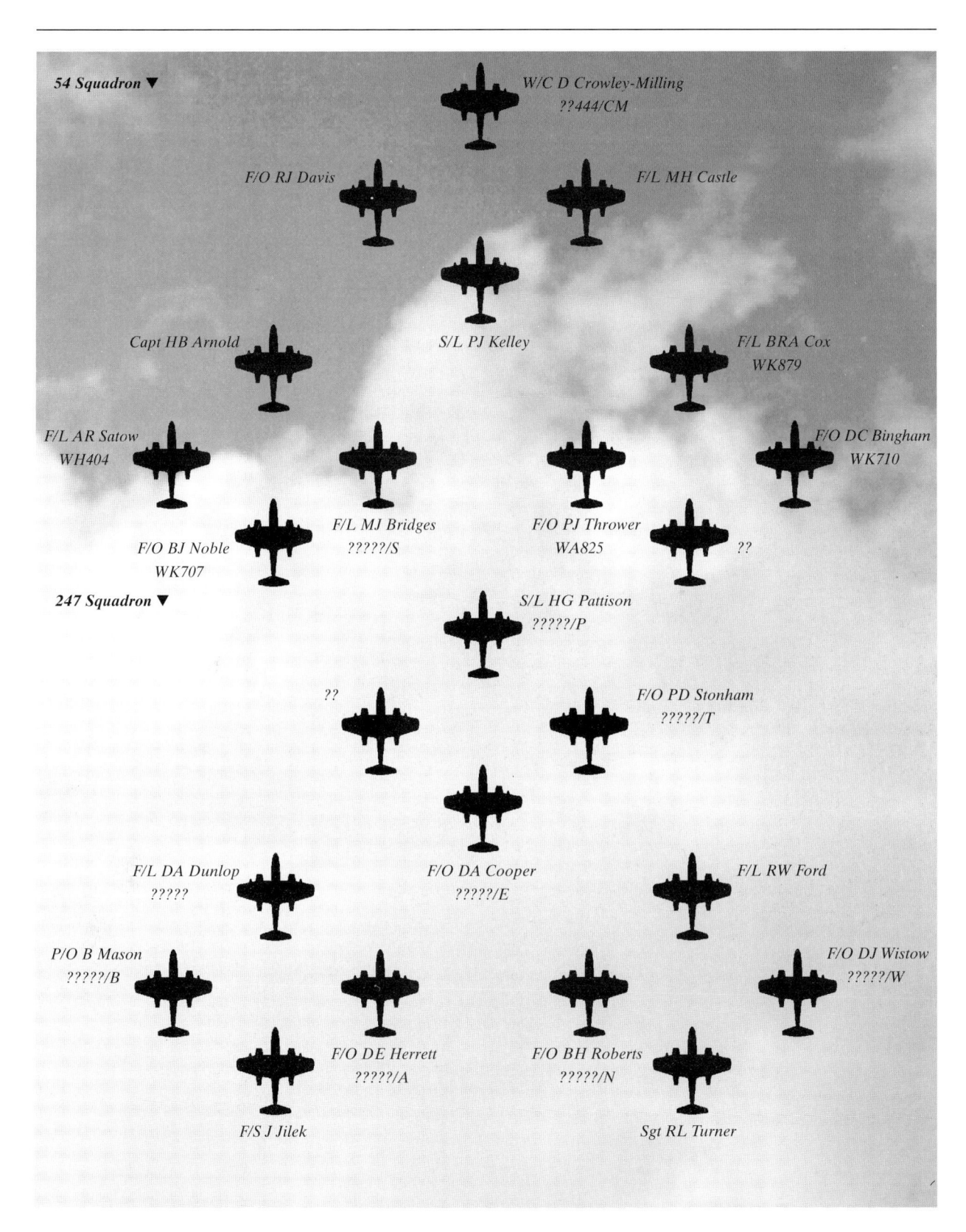

F/O PD Stonham
?????/T

F/L DA Dunlop
?????

F/O DA Cooper
?????/E

F/L RW Ford

P/O B Mason
?????/B

F/O DJ Wistow
?????/W

F/O DE Herrett
?????/A

F/O BH Roberts
?????/N

F/S J Jilek

Sgt RL Turner

FORMATION 27 ◁

2nd Tactical Air Force
25 De Havilland Venom FB.1s from 5 and 11 Squadrons, based at Wunsdorf, Germany, but operated from Wattisham

Time over Odiham: 15.55 50

Altitude: 1,100 feet

Speed: 345 mph/300 knots

FORMATION 28 ▲

Fighter Command
24 Gloster Meteor F.8s from 54 and 247 Squadrons, normally based at Odiham, but operated from Tangmere

Time over Odiham: 15.56

Altitude: 1,600 feet

Speed: 345 mph/300 knots

1 Squadron ▼

S/L JC Button

F/O DJ Seward
?????/Z

S/L RB Morison
?????/S

F/L CJ Tedder
?????/T

Sgt PJ Izzard
WA855/O

F/L JR Leask
VZ458

F/O MG King
WA854/N

F/O AGS Pattinson
?????/E

Sgt CH Maynard

F/O JM Gisborne

F/O PB Hine
WK916

F/S JC Wellby
WK908/L

FORMATION 29

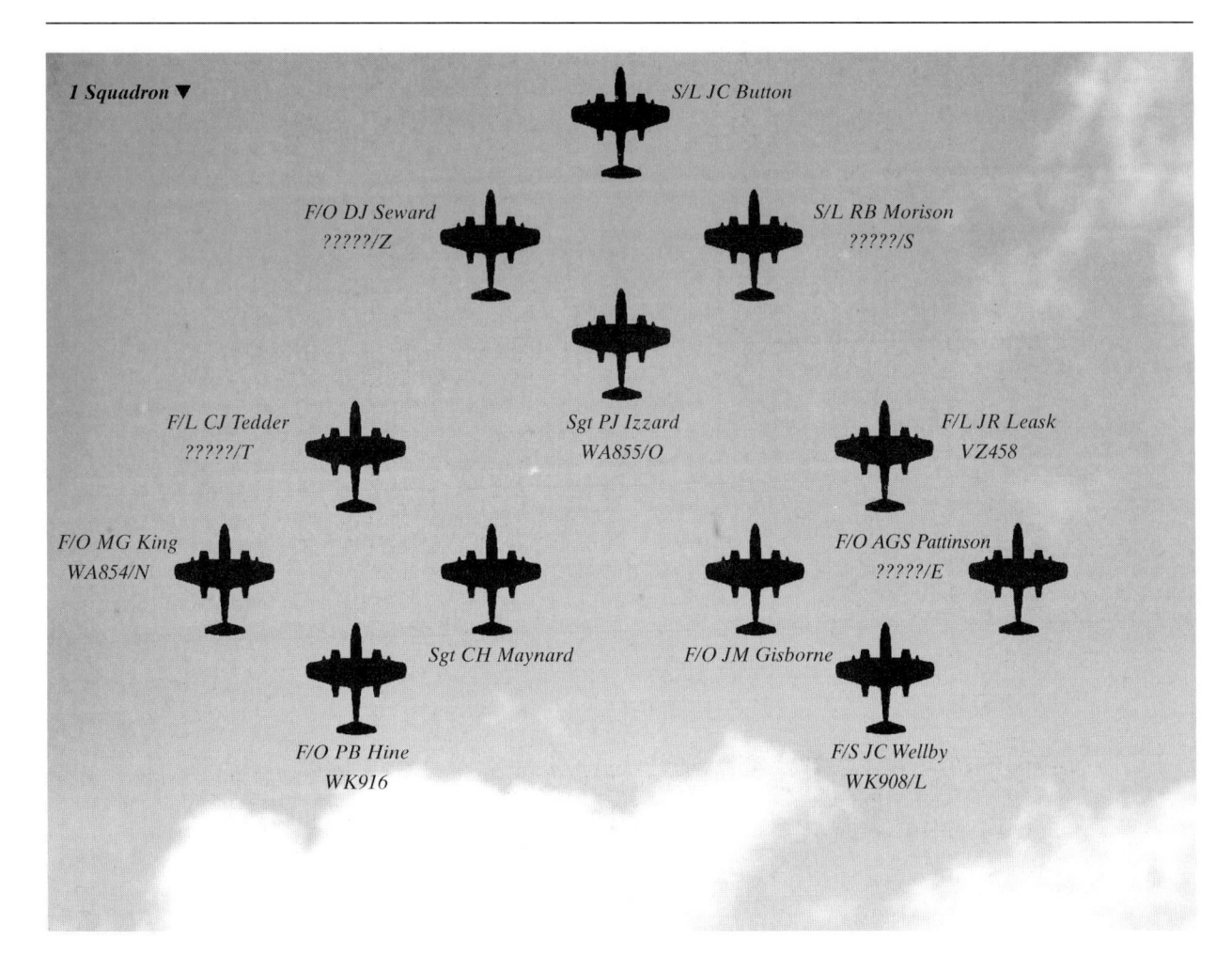

Fighter Command

24 Gloster Meteor F.8s from 1 and 41 Squadrons based at, and operated from, Biggin Hill

Time over Odiham: 15.56 50
Altitude: 1,100 feet
Speed: 345 mph 300 knots

Note: The 12 aircraft from 41 Squadron included S/L M Scannel in ?????/B; S/L WJ Hibbert (leader of one the boxes) in WE859/C; F/L JM Robertson in WE949; F/L PJ Fry in ?????/W and L Brown (No. 4 in the lead box) in ????/Y

92 Below: *Strictly speaking out of sequence, being the aircraft of Formation 33, but typical for all the Meteor formations, these are the F.8s of the Linton-on-Ouse Wing ready for takeoff*

64 Squadron ▼

W/C J Wallace

F/O C Spooner
WA896/A

S/L H Bennett

F/O AW Chambers

F/L RJ Spiers
WK968/F

F/L KVE Gilbert
WH460

P/O JW Heard
WH313/J

P/O R Dick
WK659/D

P/O RS McCarty
WH314/H

F/O RK Lord
WE926/E

F/O BW Seaman

P/O RE Holloway
??/927

65 Squadron ▼

S/L VRL Evans
?????/T

F/L DA Letham
?????/A

Sgt WB Beck

Sgt D Coupland

F/L FW Lister
?????/Q

F/L RSG Poole
?????/G

F/O DW Tanner
WE974/N

F/O SW Bainbridge
WE920/R

F/O RN Baff

Sgt GD Howarth
?????/F

F/O MC Goldsmith

Sgt JS Clanchy
VZ532

FORMATION 30

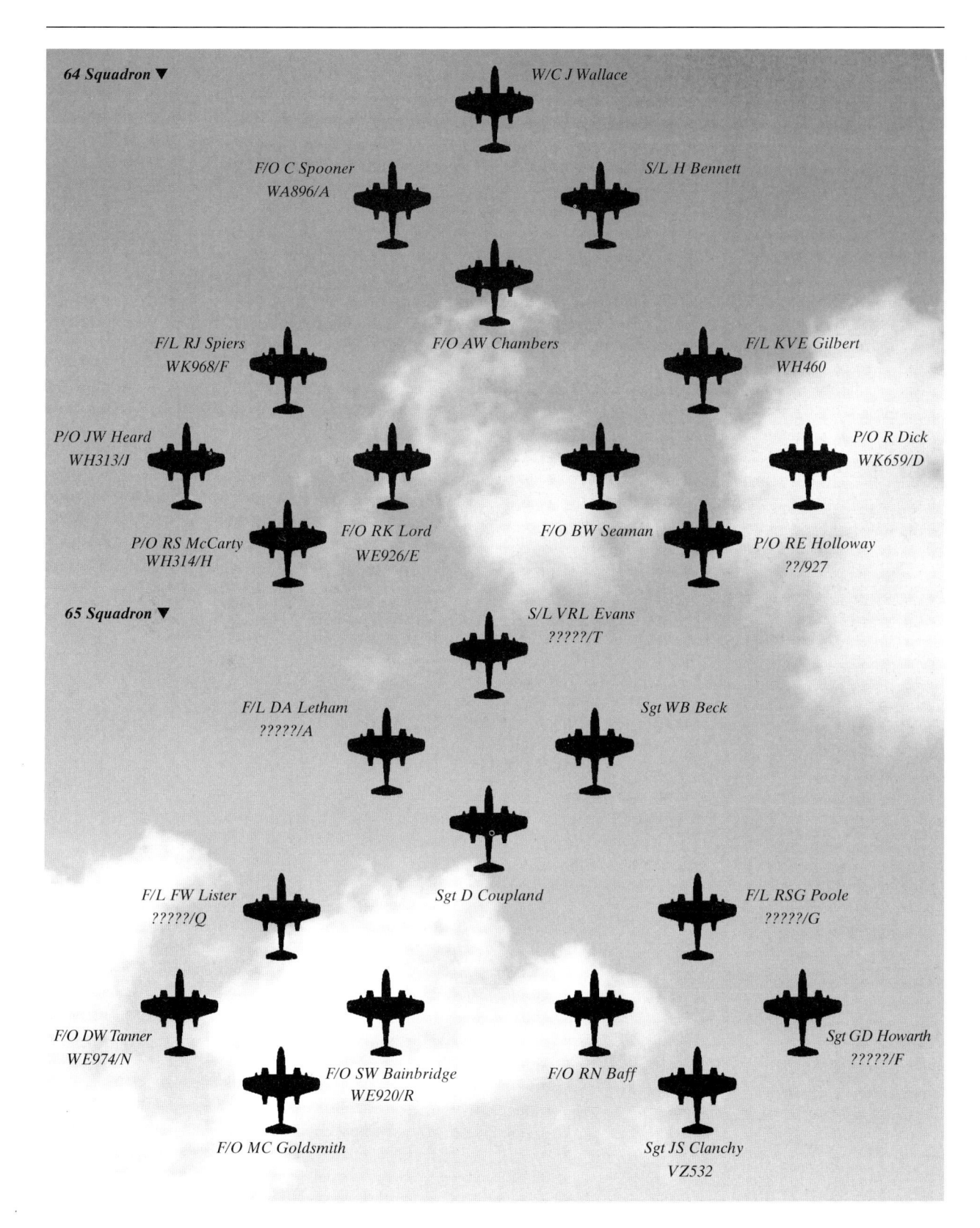

Fighter Command
24 Gloster Meteor F.8s from 64 and 65 Squadrons based at, and operated from, Duxford

Time over Odiham: 15.57
Altitude: 1,600 feet
Speed: 345 mph/300 knots

245 Squadron ▼

W/C RD Yule

F/O JL Gregg
WK893

S/L DG Ford

F/O JJ Parker
VZ565

F/L JM Nicholls
WK893

F/L EL Nieass
WK934/T

F/S BA O'Callaghan
WK936/H

F/O DH Mills
WK950/P

F/O DM Goodwin
WH416

F/O GE Williams
WK928

F/L WEA Snelling
?????/S

F/O KBE Roberts
WE901

74 Squadron ▼

Lt Col GW Mulholland

F/O D Morter
VZ529/V

F/L IAN Worby
?????/R

Sgt CG Dawson

F/L TPD Latouche
?????/Z

F/L JK Maddison
?????/B

Sgt E Noble
?????/Q

F/O GA Board

F/O PR Ward
?????/Y

Sgt R Glynn

F/O RW Napier
WF647

F/O G Thrower
WF651

FORMATION 31

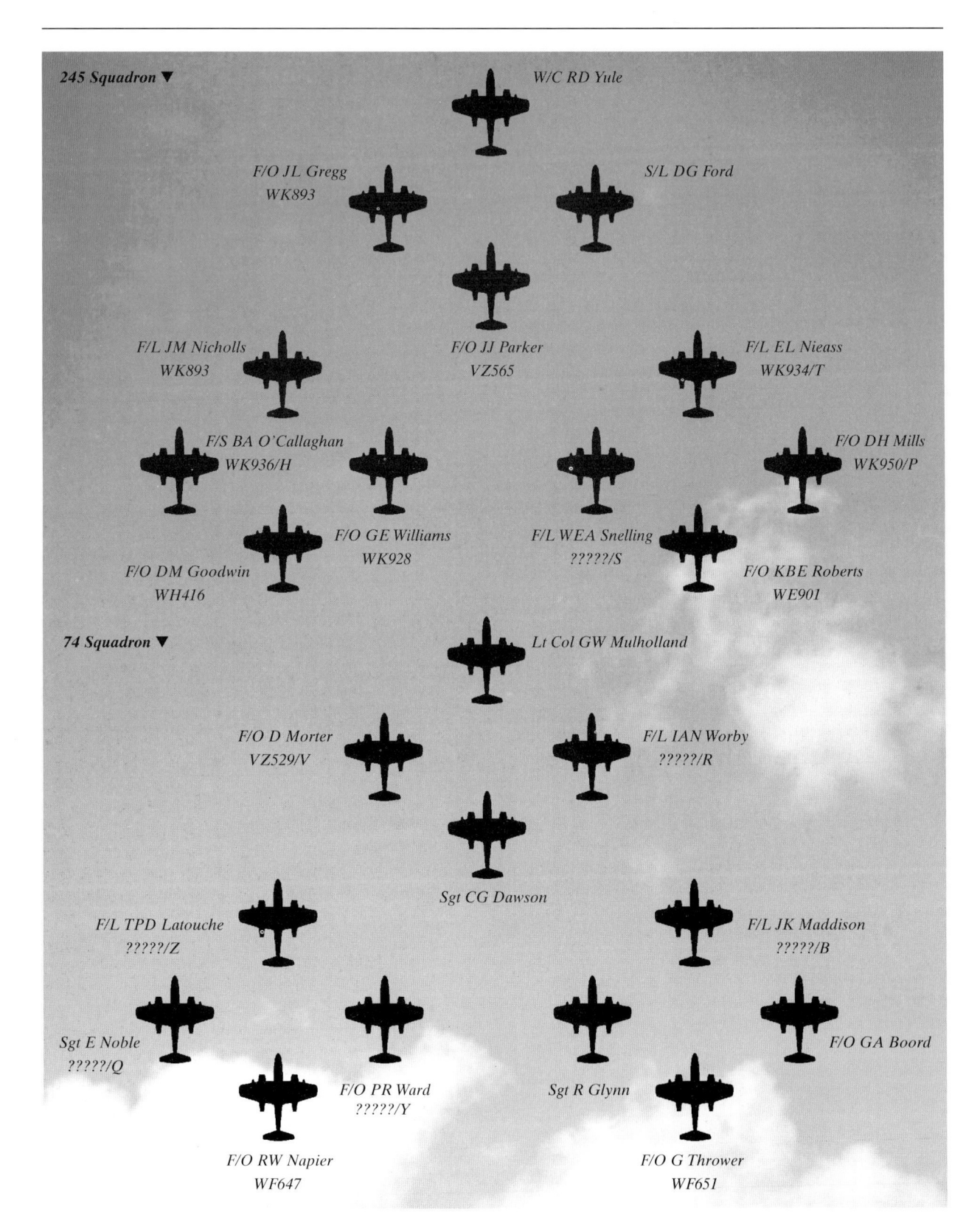

Fighter Command
24 Gloster Meteor F.8s from 74 and 245 Squadrons based at, and operated from, Horsham St Faith

Time over Odiham: 15.57.50
Altitude: 1,100 feet
Speed: 345 mph/300 knots

63 Squadron ▼

W/C PPC Barthropp
WH415/PB

S/L FW Doherty
?????/A

F/O MD Parry
??846

F/O JGF Hewitt
WE884/Y

F/L RCH Easy
WH377

F/L HJ Irving
VZ464

F/L DH Hofford
WF650

P/O D Hurley
WE852

??

F/O D Auty
??818/V

F/O KAC Wirdnam
WF705

F/O DV Tann

56 Squadron ▼

S/L RJS Spooner
?????/A

F/L JP Gledhill
WE875

F/L BPW Mercer
??905

F/O LE Clowes
??951

Capt J Bodie

F/L DPF McCaig

F/O TWA Smith

F/S NE Tindal

F/O AD Harvie

F/O S Pomfret
WA930/C

Sgt MW Warrick

F/O JH Marvin

FORMATION 32

Note: The No. 4 in the left hand box was possibly F/O P Collins or Sgt AJ McArthur

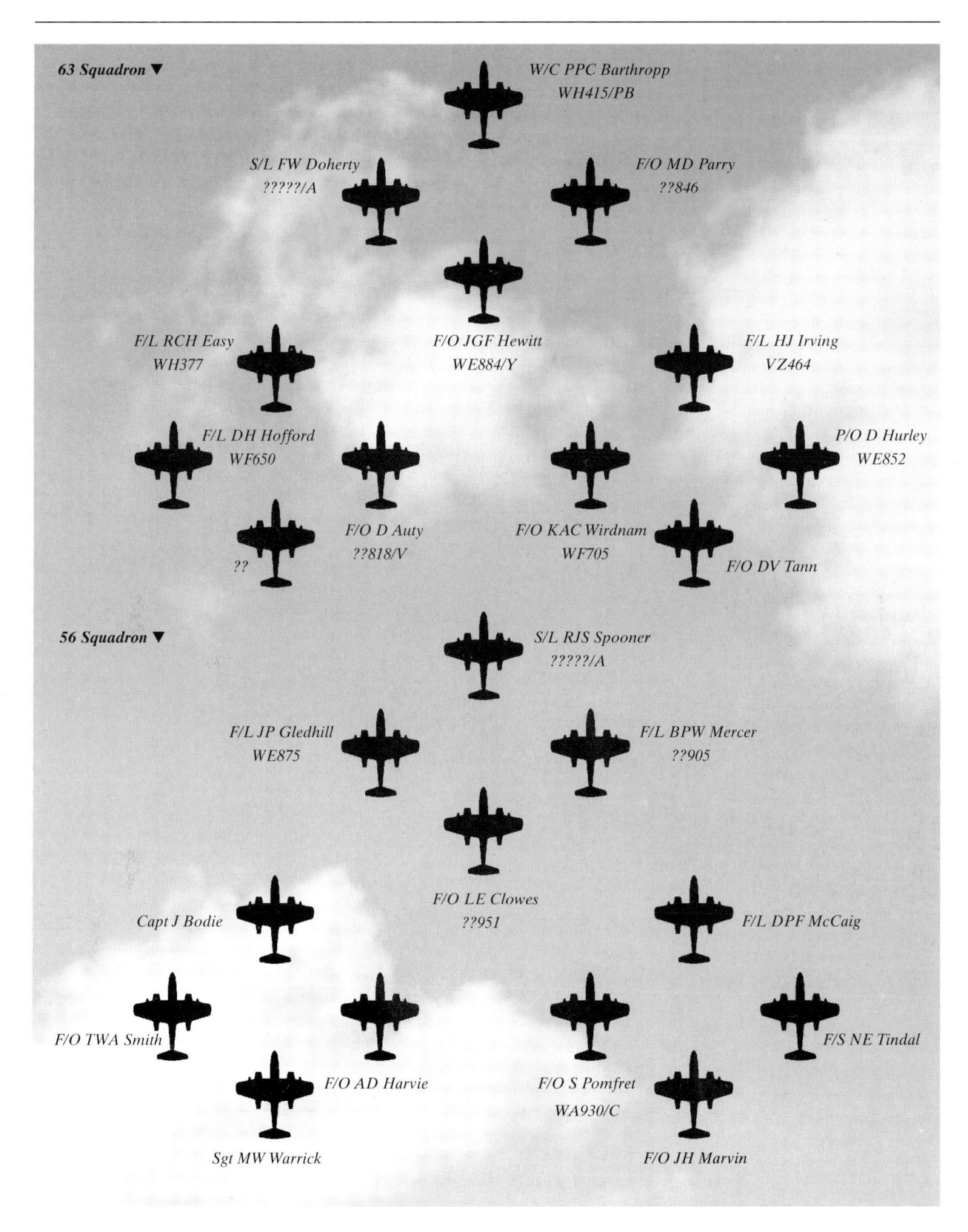

Fighter Command
24 Gloster Meteor F.8s from 56 and 63 Squadrons based at, and operated from, Waterbeach
Time over Odiham: 15.58
Altitude: 1,600 feet
Speed: 345 mph/300 knots-

77

66 Squadron ▼

W/C LA Malins
?????/LM

Sgt IH Laurie
?????/D

S/L DC Usher
?????/M

M/P J Pratt

F/S VAL Volanthen

Sgt BADM Macdonald
WF715/H

F/O R Deeley

F/L N Varanand
WK719/C

F/O DB Merifield
?????/L

F/L JD Gray

Sgt AA Holyoake
WE964/B

Sgt R Jerka

92 Squadron ▼

S/L GR Turner
WK799/A

F/L RE Dodds

F/O D Skidmore
WF711

P/O LS Naile

F/L SJ Hubbard
WF649/Z

F/L JB Jay

F/O AR Wardell

Sgt WHG Freeman
WA906

F/O CA Grabham

F/O C Walker
??813

PO R Carus-Davis
?????/S

F/O WR Webster

FORMATION 33

Note: F/L Jay and F/O Webster probably flew 'J' and 'U' respectively ('their' aircraft)

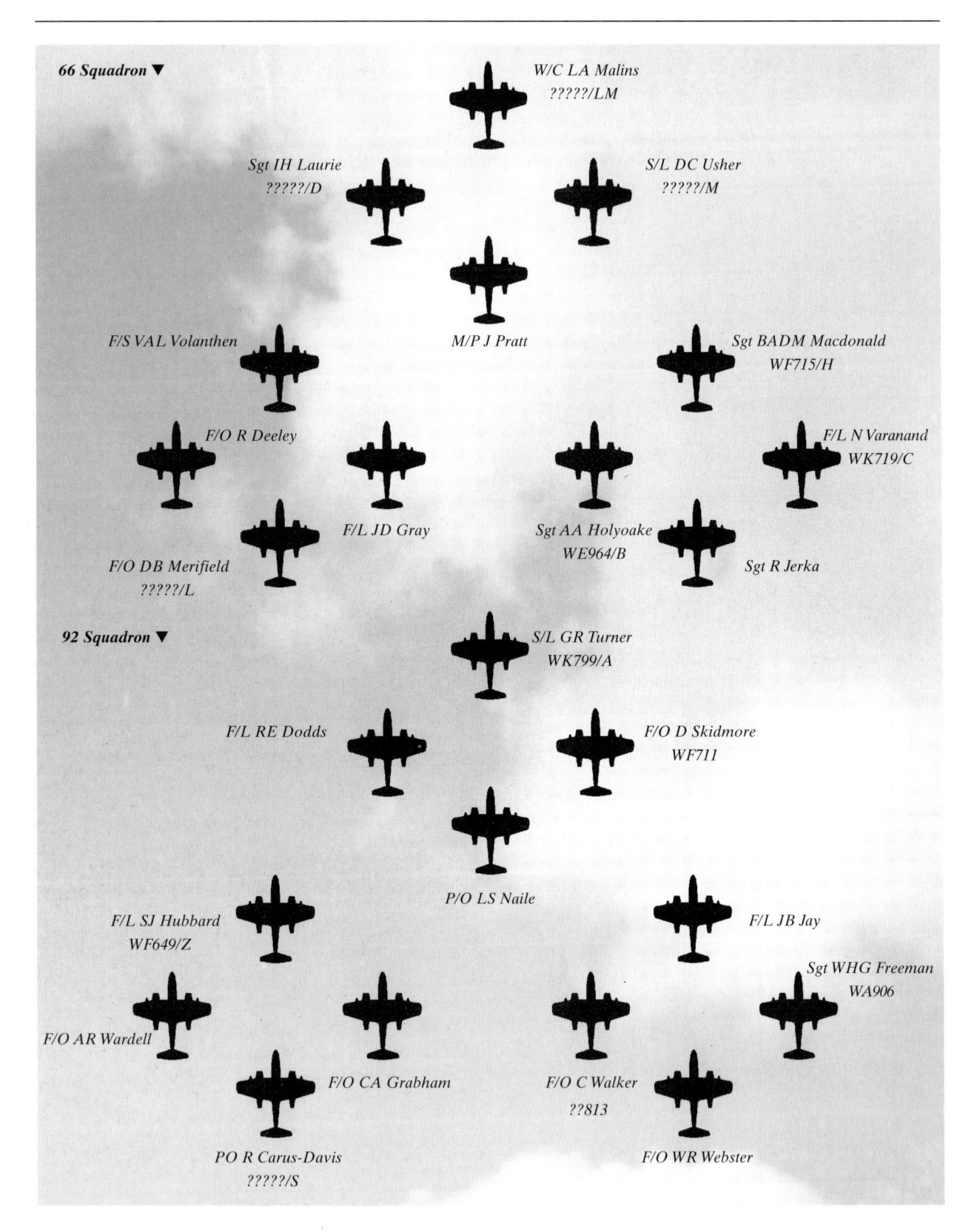

Fighter Command
24 Gloster Meteor F.8s from 66 and 92 Squadrons based at Linton-on-Ouse, operated from Honiley

Time over Odiham: 15.58 50
Altitude: 1,100 feet
Speed: 345 mph/300 knots

257 Squadron ▼

W/C LH Bartlett
??764

F/O PAL Stott
VZ471

S/L B Champneys
?????/B

F/O PG Mallett
WH291

F/O R Thomas

F/L GB Stockman

F/O MJ King
WA875

F/O FH Hartley

F/S M Jankiewicz
?????/L

F/S AE Edwards

F/O PA Roberts
?????/U

F/O R Blackburn
??444/B

263 Squadron ▼

S/L G Strange
??911

F/O GJ Bennett
WA793

F/O SB Mead
WA893

F/O PG Botterill
??484*

F/O J Birnie
?????/Z

F/L GM Hermitage
WH299

F/L RS May

F/O L Scott
??959

F/O WJ Elford

F/O BC Mills

F/O NRC Price
WA986

F/L DJ Rhodes

FORMATION 34

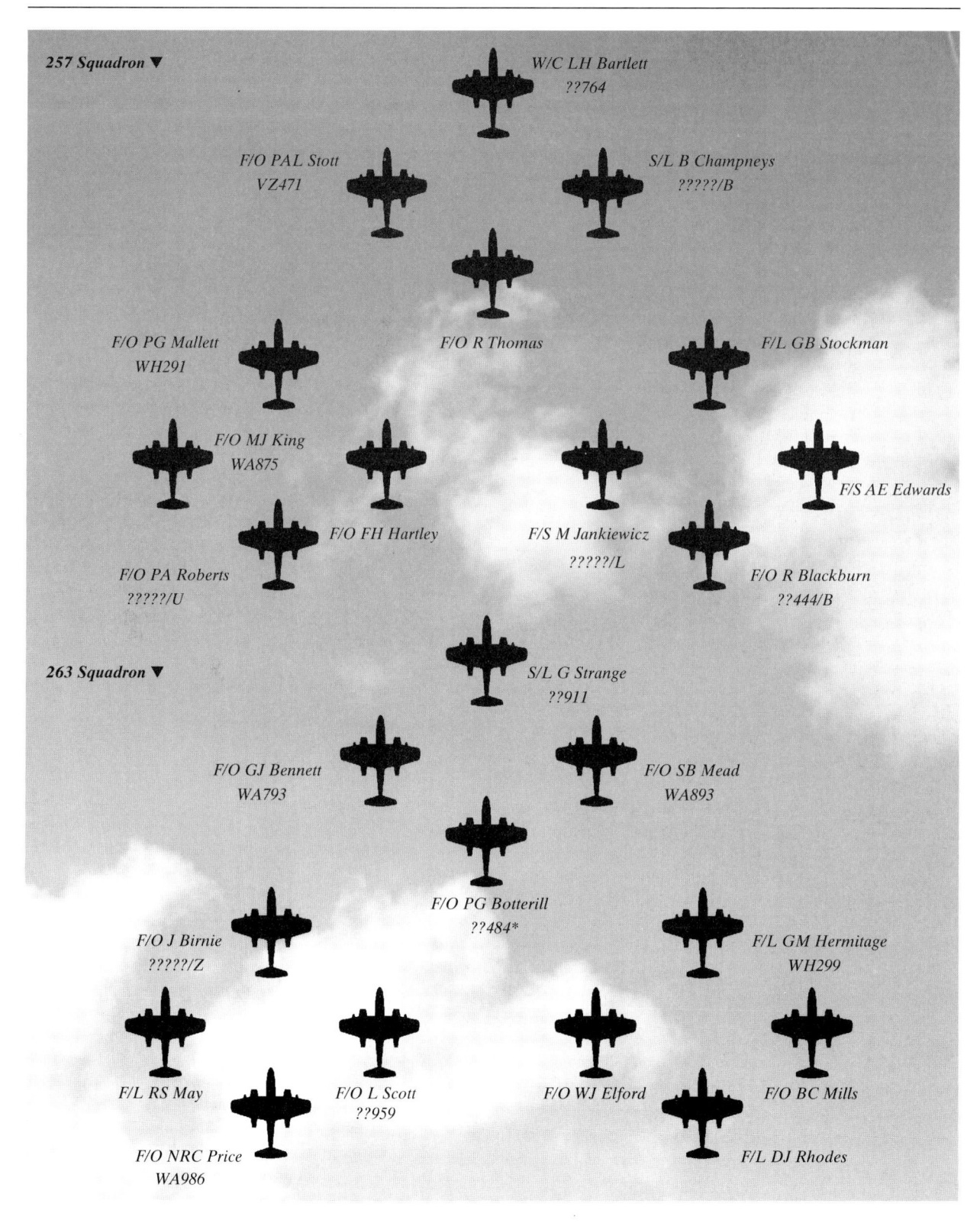

Fighter Command

24 Gloster Meteor F.8s from 257 and 263 Squadrons based at, and operated from, Wattisham

Time over Odiham: 15.59
Altitude: 1,600 feet
Speed: 345 mph/300 knots

Notes: F/L Bowen flew WH258 with 257 Squadron as 'B' Flight Commander, having transferred from 64 Squadron due to the collision on 8 July. Perhaps he replaced F/L Stockman

The 'B' flown by S/L Champneys was possibly a borrowed aircraft, or may be an example of duplicate codes (see Appendix 1 on Page 90)

*F/O Botterill's logbook shows WA484. The most likely candidate is WH484 borrowed from 64 Squadron. The 64 Squadron Operations Record Book says that the ground crews produced the whole Squadron of 17 aircraft. Sixteen got airborne, including the T.7 and three spare F.8s. The seventeenth went on a minor inspection a few minutes before the others took-onff. Normally each squadron took only 2 spare aircraft. 263 borrowed WK865 from North Weald. It was picked up by F/O Price on the morning of 15 July, and returned the following day

43 Squadron ▼

W/C PGH Matthews
?????/PM

F/O DH Ross

S/L RE Lelong
WA794

F/O G Rorison
WA847/P

F/L S Walker
????/W

F/L JA Jackson
WK859

F/O HJ Gourley

F/O CA Simpson
?????/H

Sgt H Watt

F/L RSM Dadd
?????/O

Sgt R Ross

Sgt GG Smith

222 Squadron ▼

S/L RK Wilson

Sgt AIS Donald
????/U

F/L W Hughes
VZ554

F/L K Burge
WA933/P

F/S RPF Hill
WK861

F/L DT Adamson
VZ448/A

F/O BE Allen
WK918

F/O J Sutton
WK921

F/O WW Ferguson
VZ523/Q

F/O S Wood

F/O GRG Smith
VZ515/F

F/S A Piercy
VZ516

FORMATION 35

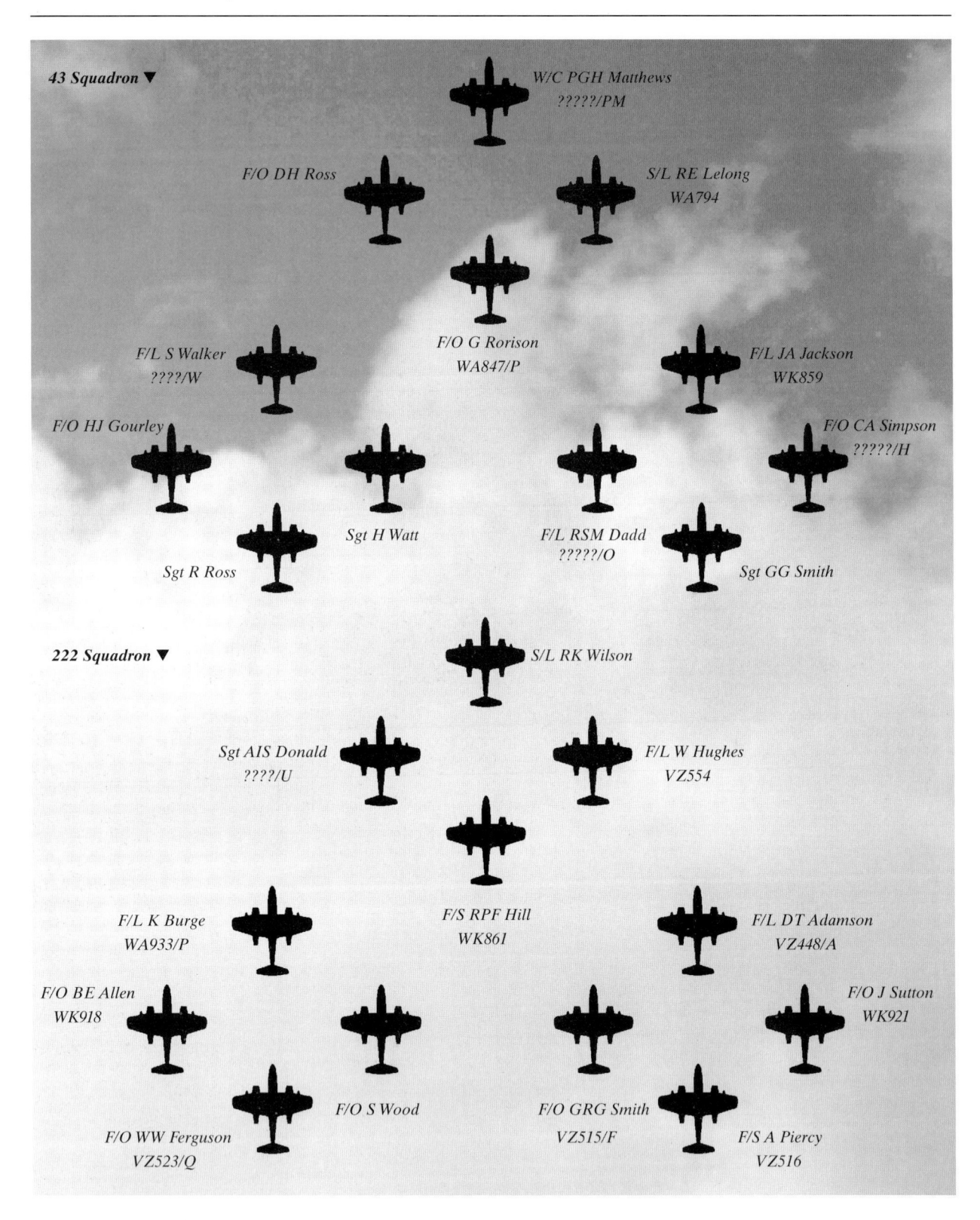

Fighter Command
24 Gloster Meteor F.8s from 43 and 222 Squadrons based at Leuchars, operated from Wymeswold
Time over Odiham: 15.59.50
Altitude: 1,100 feet
Speed: 345 mph/300 knots

72 Squadron ▼

W/C RW Oxspring
WF677/RWO

F/L FR James
WK656

F/O DP Carey*

F/O JS Chambers

F/L H Minnis
??691/X

S/L TD Sanderson
????/E

F/L AT Shaw

F/O DJ Keats
WH463

F/O JG Cruse
?????/R

F/L MJ Woodyer

Sgt JF Joachim

F/O AJ Robson

19 Squadron ▼

S/L B Beard
??348

Sgt JJFM Logan
WA758

F/O D Turgoose
WE855

F/O TJ Cresswell
WA816/M

F/L CRG Neville
WK734

F/L JA Stephen
????/H

F/O BA Smith

P/O EW Hopkins
WE863/A

F/O FR Pearson
WE857/P

F/O A Goadby
WB109/R

F/O ST Jenkins

F/O JA Harrison
WB108

FORMATION 36

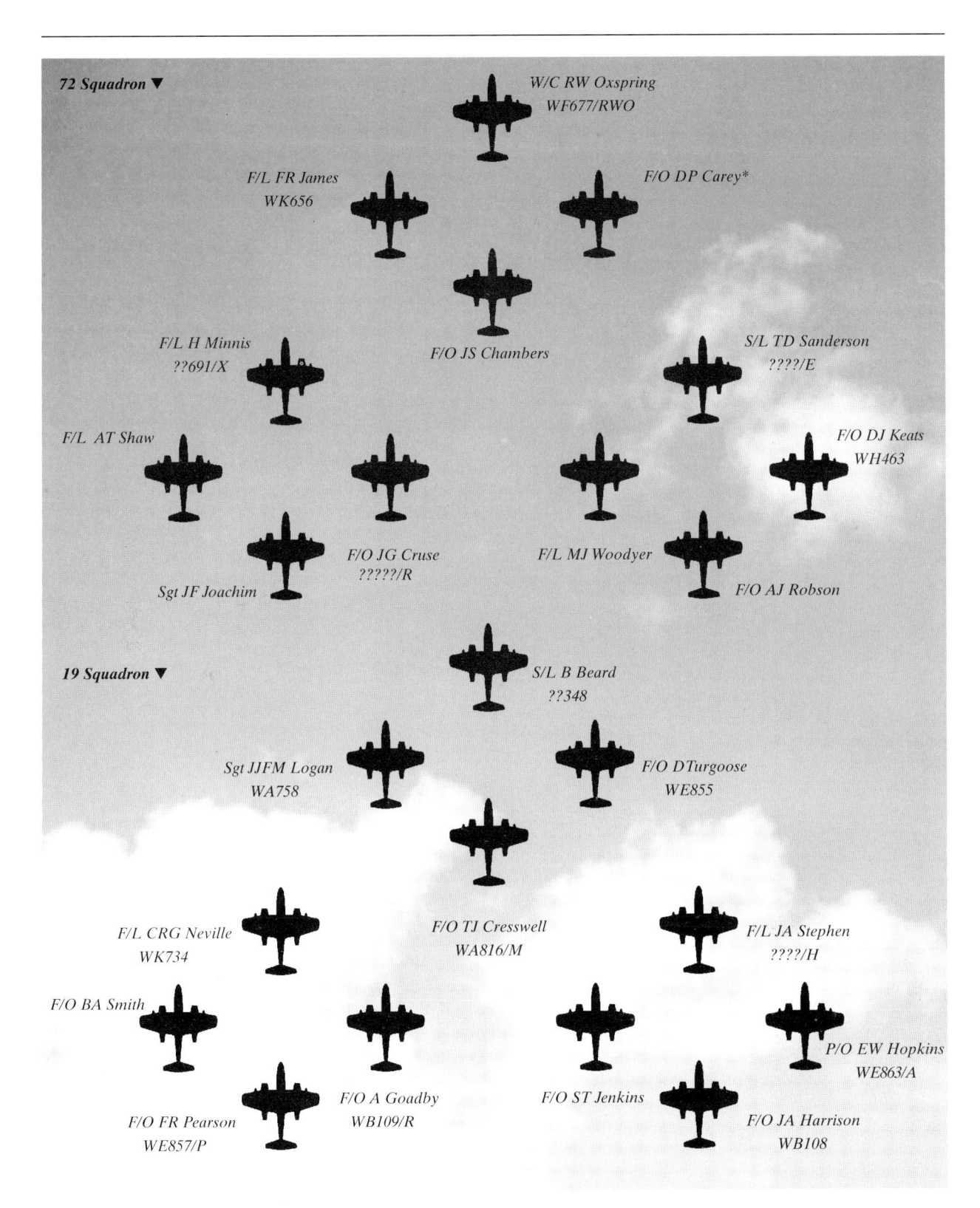

Fighter Command

24 Gloster Meteor F.8s from 19 and 72 Squadrons based at Church Fenton, operated from North Weald

Time over Odiham: 16.00
Altitude: 1,600 feet
Speed: 345 mph/300 knots

Note: *F/O Carey probably flew VZ525/N ('his' aircraft)

81

85 Squadron ▼

W/C AP Dotteridge
F/O Harty
WM154

F/L AJ Mackinnon
WD620

S/L JD Hawkins
F/L A Devine
??763

F/L WE Hedley
F/O PJ Wilde
WM175

F/L CJ Holmes
F/L JH Bransgrove
WM177

P/O WW Hill
??614

F/O RF Cooper
F/O M Hart
??615

F/L AS Button
WD618

F/O KC Povey
Mr Baxter
WM174

29 Squadron ▼

S/L EB Sismore
WD722

F/L EA Devillez
F/O Holden
?????/W

F/L JM Hocking
F/O Sheppard
WD600

F/L NCP Baddin
F/O McLean
WD599/P

F/L LR Schofield
F/L Davis
WD603/C

F/O AN Jones

F/O RH Bateman
WD792

F/O AEG Abczynski

Sgt EIV Lee

FORMATION 37

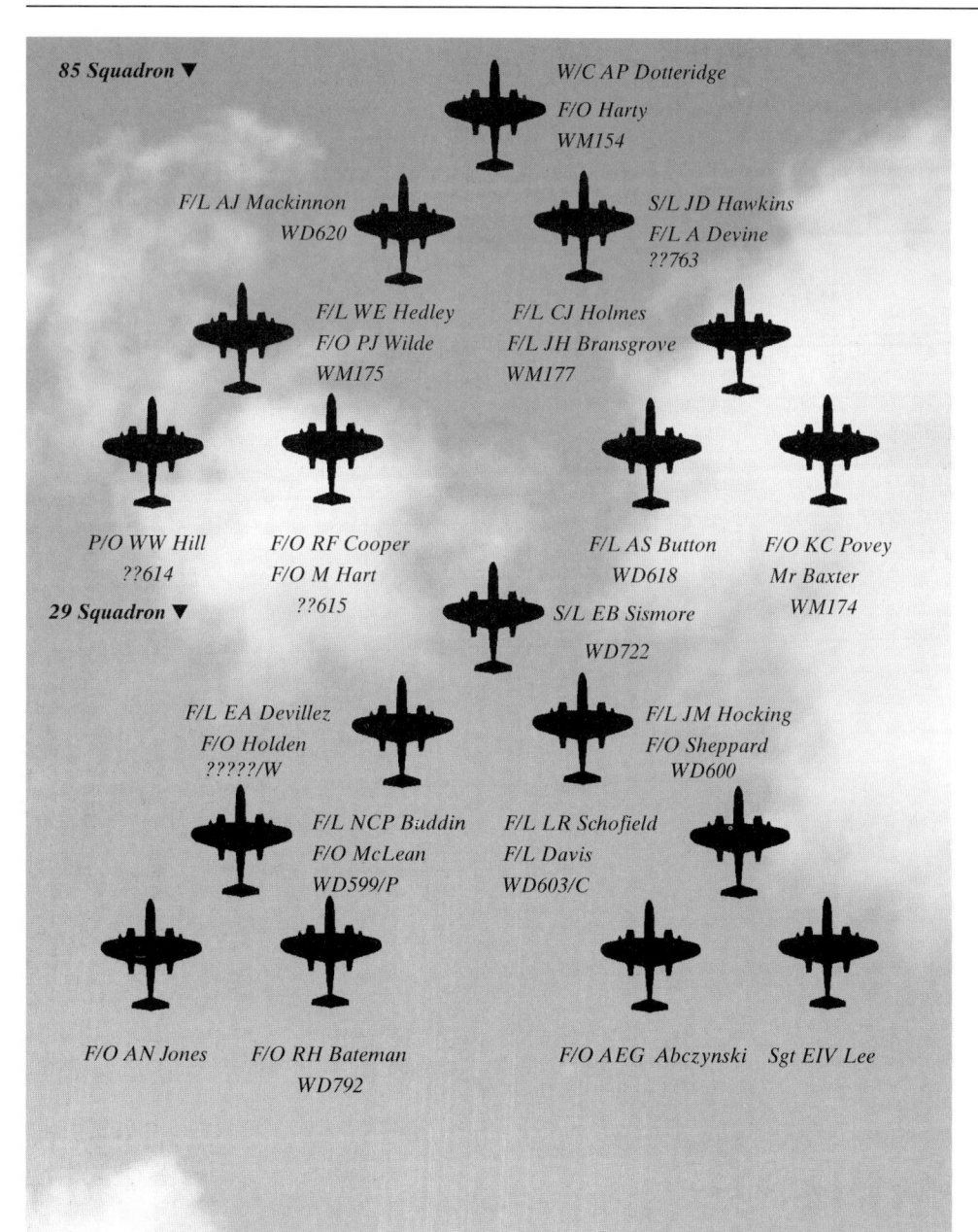

Fighter Command
18 Gloster Meteor NF.11s from 85 and 29 Squadrons, both operated from West Malling. 85 Squadron's home base, while 29 Squadron was based at Tangmere

Time over Odiham: 16.00 50
Altitude: 1,100 feet
Speed: 345 mph/300 knots

94: *Gloster Meteor WM237/S of 228 OCU in the static display showing the typical night fighter camouflage of Medium Sea Grey and Dark Green sported by almost all aircraft of the type*

FORMATION 38

Fighter Command
18 Gloster Meteor NF.11s from 141 and 264 Squadrons, both operated from West Malling. 141 Squadron's home base was Coltishall, while 264 was normally housed at Linton-on-Ouse

Time over Odiham: 16.01
Altitude: 1,600 feet
Speed: 345 mph/300 knots

Notes: 151 Squadron (based at Leuchars) provided the missing vics in the 141 and 264 squadron formations. The positions are not known, but those known to have taken part included: S/L AD Boyle and F/L KB Wright in ??270; F/O AW Mutch and F/O VJ Morgan in WD787; F/L RS Peters and F/O GJB Claridge in ?????/E; F/L B Appleyard in WD629; F/O JE George in ?????/K

95 Below: *Meteor NF.11s of assorted MUs—the nearest three being from 8 MU, machines from 38 MU behind*

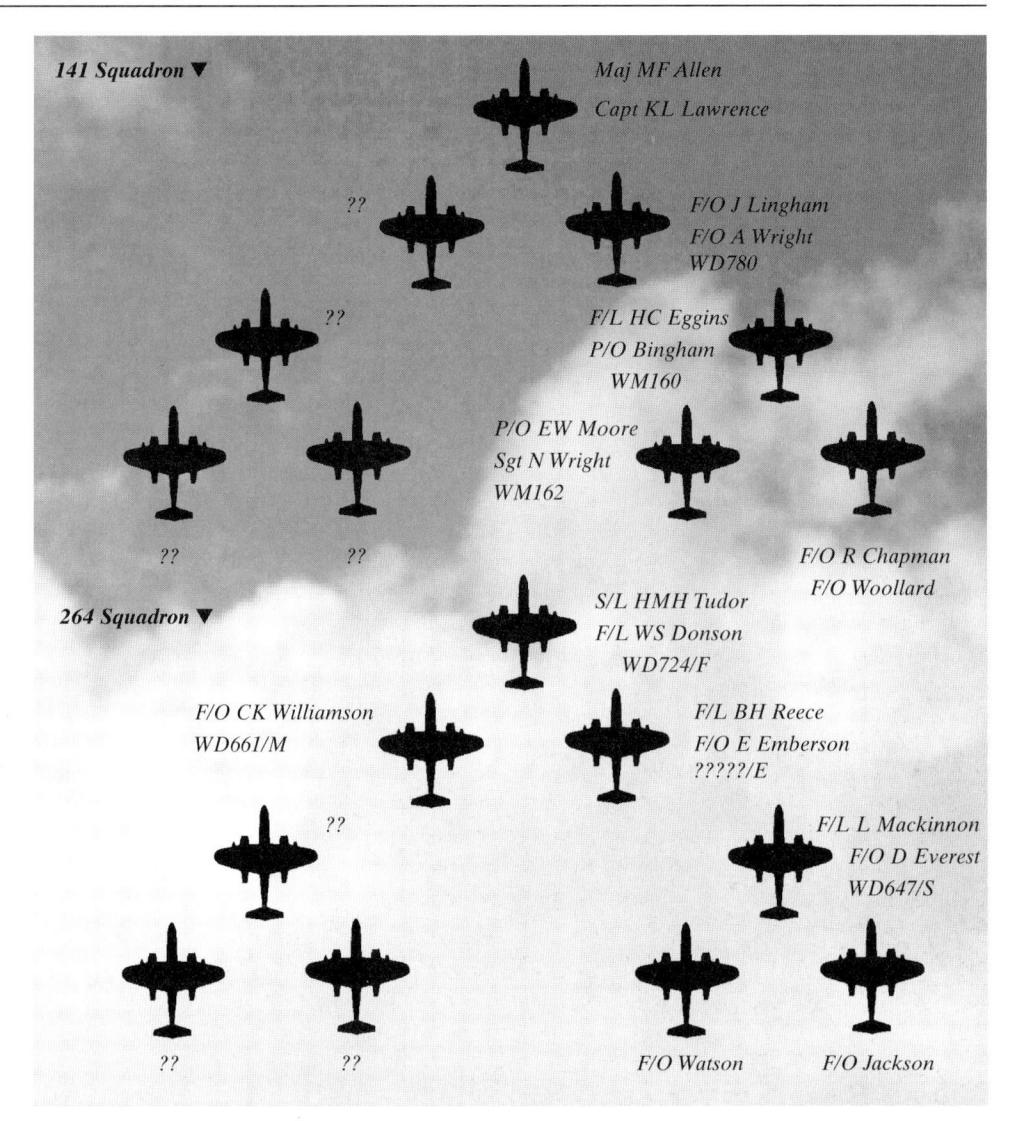

141 Squadron ▼

Maj MF Allen
Capt KL Lawrence

??

F/O J Lingham
F/O A Wright
WD780

??

F/L HC Eggins
P/O Bingham
WM160

P/O EW Moore
Sgt N Wright
WM162

F/O R Chapman
F/O Woollard

??   ??

264 Squadron ▼

S/L HMH Tudor
F/L WS Donson
WD724/F

F/O CK Williamson
WD661/M

F/L BH Reece
F/O E Emberson
?????/E

??

F/L L Mackinnon
F/O D Everest
WD647/S

??   ??   F/O Watson   F/O Jackson

[Formation diagram with aircraft positions:]

- G/C NC Hyde, WH706, 617 Squadron
- S/L JS Millington, WD996, 12 Squadron
- S/L JCM Mountford, WE111, 9 Squadron
- F/O J Bush, ??653, 50 Squadron

9 Squadron ▼
- S/L SG Hewitt, WF908
- Sgt KS Neate / Sgt Holland, WD998
- Sgt AD Platt, WD997
- F/L EJG Flavell, WD999

- F/O BW Scott, WD941

101 Squadron ▼
- F/L NA Caillard, WD934
- F/L K Wightman, WD948
- F/O JG Kemp, WD949

- S/L JS Owen, ??536
- F/L JE Smith, ??647
- S/L J Crampton, WD936, 101 Squadron
- F/L FA Thomas, ??652

12 Squadron ▼
- Maj FE Singleton, WD993
- Sgt MJ Hawkins, WH662
- F/L JGW Stroud, WF891
- F/O J Cochrane, WD955
- F/L GO Russell, WH659

617 Squadron ▼
- S/L D Roberts, WH854
- F/L J Gale, WD982
- S/L WD Robertson, WD995, 101 Squadron

FORMATION 39

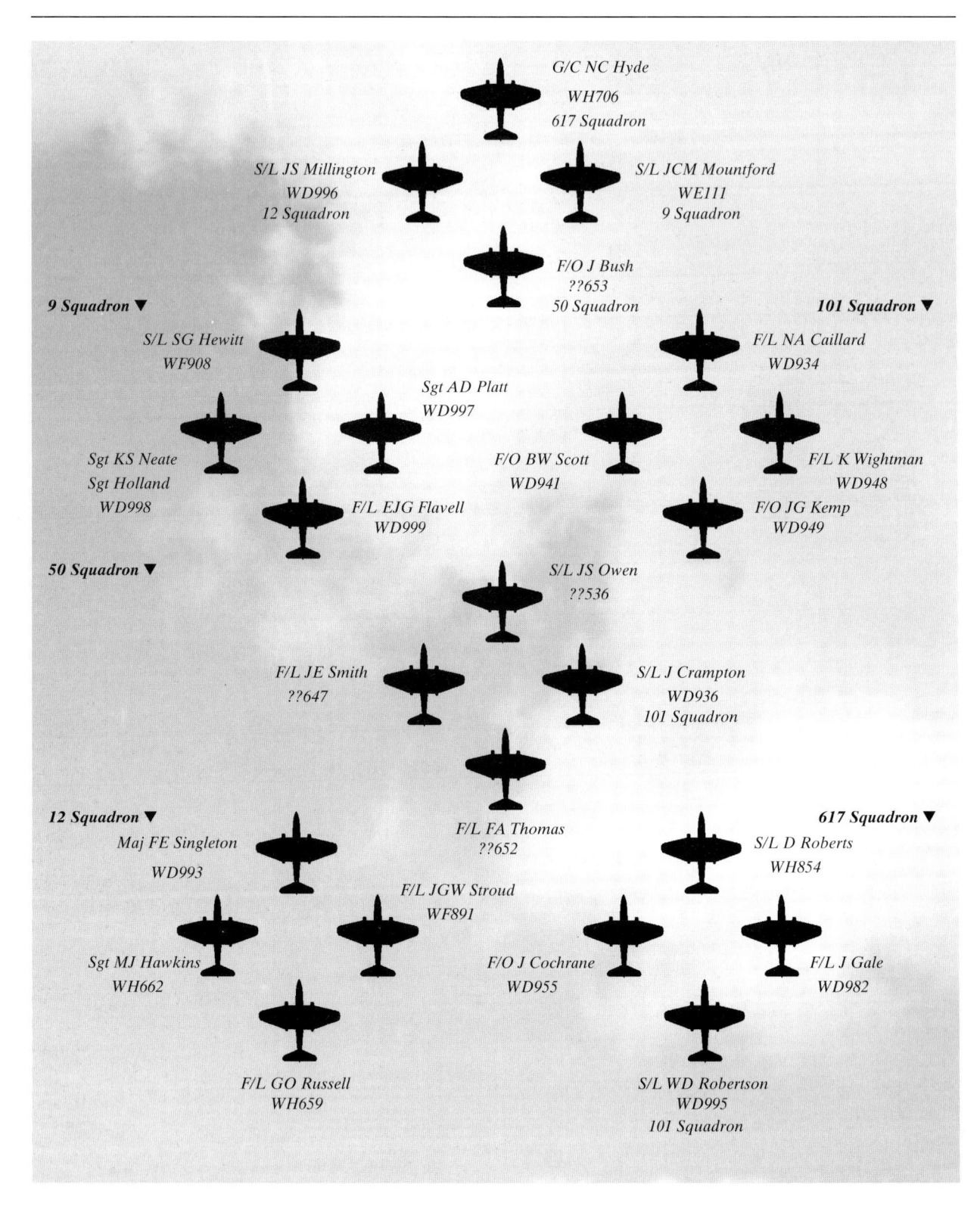

Bomber Command

24 English Electric Canberra B.2s from 9, 12, 50, 101 and 617 Squadrons, operated from Binbrook

Time over Odiham: 16.01.50
Altitude: 1,100 feet
Speed: 345 mph/300 knots

Notes: Serials come from the Form 541 record. The second No. 2 box has some changes: S/L Robertson's logbook shows that he flew WD995 of 617 Squadron although he had just become CO of 101 Squadron. F/O Dowling's logbook says he took part in this position in WD980, but the Form 541 records him as a spare

The record cards show the following serials for 50 Squadron: WH647, WH652, WH653 and XA536

The following are confirmed from pilots' logbooks: WD934, WD936, WD955, WD980, WD982, WD995, WD997, WD998, WD999 (shown in the Form 541 records as WP514), WF908, WH659, WH706 and XA536

Photos taken on 15 July confirm WD934 and WE111. The other serials are indistinct, but what can be seen confirms the layout above

109 Squadron ▼

S/L JES Hill
WF915

Capt MLW Peters
WE115

F/L RS Nichol
WE117

F/L JG Wynne
WF914

139 Squadron ▼

F/L G Price
WH645
109 Squadron

F/L EG Jones
WJ971
139 Squadron

F/L GA Francis
WH658

??
WH728

F/O PJ Clarke
WH656

F/O PHJ Butler
WH651

??
WH730

F/L RGM Burton
WH655

231 OCU ▼

W/C R Macfarlane
WH704

F/L KC Howard
?????

F/L JV Horwood
WF913

M/P AV Potter
WD981

10 Squadron ▼

S/L DR Howard
WH672

231 OCU ▼

G/C GK Buckingham
?????

Sgt DV Brice
WH665

F/L RG Collins
WH667

F/O RI Young
WD966

F/S A Ramsden
WF910

F/L RJE Wareham
WH674

F/L KW Rogers
??120

FORMATION 40

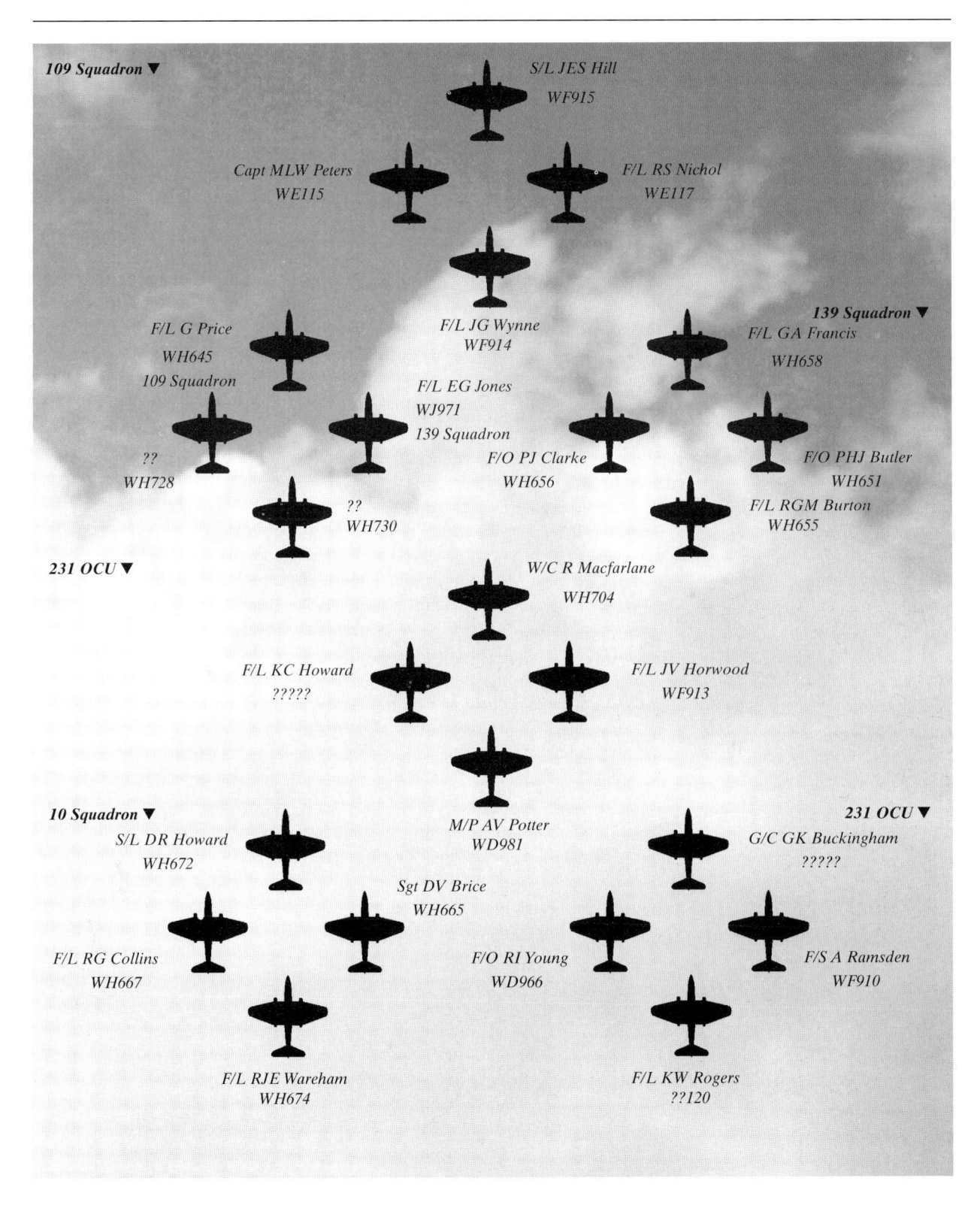

Bomber Command

24 English Electric Canberra B.2s from 10, 109 and 139 Squadrons and 231 Operational Conversion Unit, operated from Hemswell and Scampton

Time over Odiham: 16.02
Altitude: 1,600 feet
Speed: 345 mph/300 knots

Notes: The OCU aircraft serials come from pilots' logbooks except for WH704. The 10, 109 and 139 Squadron aircraft serials come from the Form 541 Records

A photo taken on 15 July confirms the serials of the 109 Squadron box and that the 139 Squadron box serials begin with 'WH'. It also confirms the other box includes WH645 and WJ971 and that Nos. 3 and 4 (WH728 and WH730 respectively) are from 27 Squadron. The Bentley Priory record has F/S JR Foster in No. 3 position (WH644 of 109 Squadron from the Form 541 record), but this was presumably a spare. The same record does not indicate anyone in the No. 4 slot. In the second formation of 12 aircraft, a photo shows WH704 as the leader, and confirms WE120, WF913 and those in the 10 Squadron box

85

3 Squadron ▼

W/C MH Le Bas
XB619

F/L TP Fargher
?????

F/L V Woods
XB678

F/O JC Sprent
XB726

F/L TA Warren
?????

S/L WJS Sutherland
?????

F/O AWA Wright
XB633/W

F/O KD Crisp
XB536

F/O J Bruce
?????/P

Sgt JK Chappell
XB740

F/O LD Day
XB590/V

Sgt GH Cole
XB617

67 Squadron ▼

F/L J Mellers
XB688

S/L W Harbison
??639

P/O DB Birley
?????/B

F/L AGS Wilson
?????

P/O JSD Craig
XB690/Z

F/L AH Turner
XB737/A

F/O DJ Elsden
XB598/R

F/L PKV Hicks
XB674

F/L D Mullarkey
?????/V

F/O JT Reynolds
XB586/X

P/O DG Riley
XB700/T

P/O MJC Grant
?????

FORMATION 41

2nd Tactical Air Force

24 Canadair Sabre F.4s from 3 and 67 Squadron, both based at Wildenrath, Germany, but operated from Duxford

Time over Odiham: 16.02.50
Altitude: 1,100 feet
Speed: 345 mph/300 knots

Notes: F/L Warren probably flew 'Y' ('his' aircraft)

C. Alsop flew XB612, probably as a spare

F/L Woods flew XB678 of 67 Squadron—he was Deputy Leader, so was probably with 67 Squadron

Royal Canadian Air Force
441 Squadron ➤
439 Squadron ▼

F/L NA Burns
19167

410 Squadron ▼

F/O DC McIlraith
19154

F/O DR Williamson
19149

F/L R Morris
?????

F/O HR Wingate
?????

F/O EN Ronaasen
?????

F/O WH Thompson
?????

F/O WG McEwen
19173

F/O RM Bradley
19166

F/O HC Ruecker
19138

F/O RR Biggar
?????

F/O HF Reischman
?????

S/L WTH Gill
?????

441 Squadron ➤
439 Squadron ▼

F/L J Villeneuve
19183

??
?????

410 Squadron ▼

F/L GH Nichols
19180

F/L HF Wenz
19205

F/O RB Haverstock
?????

F/O RM Knox-Leet
?????

F/O RS Poole
19171

F/O JS Hannah
19114

F/O NM Mackerracher
?????

F/O RJM Haran
19186

F/O MW Sills
?????

F/L DH Atherton
?????

441 Squadron ➤
439 Squadron ▼

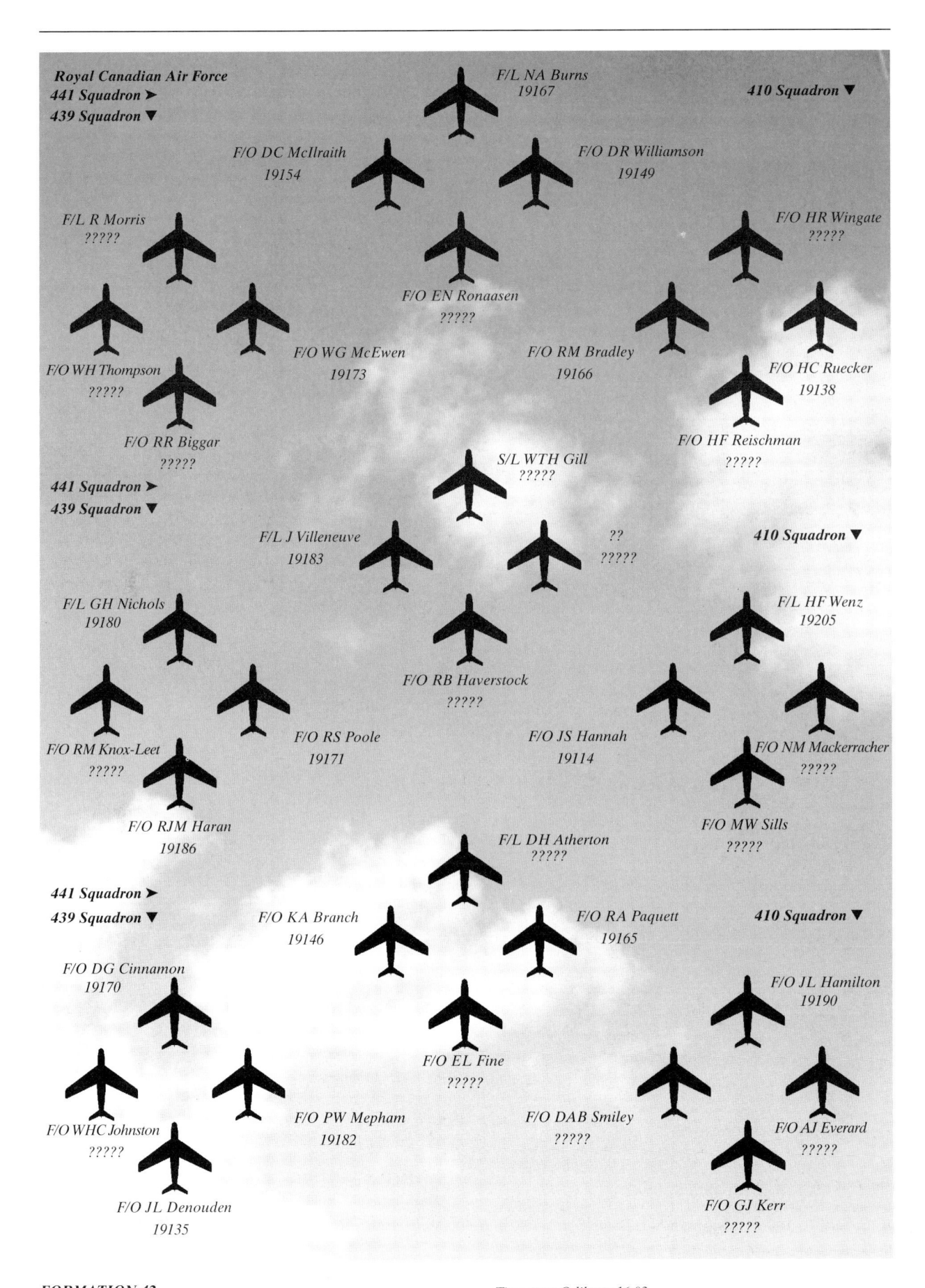

F/O KA Branch
19146

F/O RA Paquett
19165

410 Squadron ▼

F/O DG Cinnamon
19170

F/O JL Hamilton
19190

F/O EL Fine
?????

F/O WHC Johnston
?????

F/O PW Mepham
19182

F/O DAB Smiley
?????

F/O AJ Everard
?????

F/O JL Denouden
19135

F/O GJ Kerr
?????

FORMATION 42
Royal Canadian Air Force

36 Canadair F.2 Sabres of 410, 439 and 441 Squadrons, operated from North Luffenham

Time over Odiham: 16.03
Altitude: 1,600 feet
Speed: 345 mph/300 knots

96: *The 36 Canadair Sabre F.2s of the Royal Canadian Air Force strolling past at 300 knots*

FORMATION 43

A&AEE Boscombe Down
6 Supermarine Swift F.1s operated from Boscombe Down

Time over Odiham: 16.03 50
Altitude: 1,100 feet
Speed: 460 mph/400 knots

Notes: An article by A Curry and F Goodridge in Flypast *magazine of May 1987 notes that prototype WJ965 and five production Swift F.1s (WK194-WK197 and WK200) took part on 15 July*

An indistinct photo taken on 15 July helps to confirm WJ965 and suggests that F/L Burton's aircraft was WK195

F/L Burton
?????

F/L AF Jenkins
WJ965

W/C T Balmforth
WK196

F/L MT Harding-Rolls
WK200

S/L CS Hunton
WK197

S/L NED Lewis
?????

FORMATION 44

Ministry of Supply
The first Handley Page Victor prototype WB771, operated from Radlett and flown by S/L HG Hazledon

Time over Odiham: 16.04 50
Altitude: 1,600 feet
Speed: 288 mph/250 knots

FORMATION 45

Ministry of Supply
The second Vickers Valiant prototype WB215, operated from Wisley and flown by EB Trubshaw

Time over Odiham: 16.05
Altitude: 1,600 feet
Speed: 345 mph/300 knots

FORMATION 46

Ministry of Supply
The first Avro Vulcan prototype, VX770, operated from Woodford and flown by W/C RJ Falk

Time over Odiham: 16.05 50
Altitude: 1,600 feet
Speed: 460 mph/400 knots

FORMATION 47

Ministry of Supply
The third Gloster Javelin prototype, WT827, operated from Moreton Valence and flown by S/L WA Waterton

Time over Odiham: 16.06
Altitude: 1,100 feet
Speed: 575 mph/500 knots

FORMATION 48

Ministry of Supply
The first production Hawker Hunter F.1, WT555, operated from Dunsfold and flown by S/L NF Duke

Time over Odiham: 16.06 50
Altitude: 1,100 feet
Speed: 668 mph/580 knots

FORMATION 49

Ministry of Supply
The Supermarine Swift F.4 prototype, WK198, flown from Chilbolton by Lt Cdr MJ Lithgow

Time over Odiham: 16.07
Altitude: 1,100 feet
Speed: 668 mph/580 knots

Notes: The aircraft suffered an engine seizure after the flypast and was 'dead-stick' landed at Chilbolton

AIRCRAFT AND MEN

The following lists detail some of the units involved in the Flypast.

The serials are taken from the Record Cards held at the Royal Air Force Museum, Hendon, and show those aircraft on strength on 15 July 1953.

The codes are taken from records supplied by Geoff Cruikshank, the late John Rawlings, Ray Sturtivant and Roger Lindsay, supplemented/corrected from Pilot Logbook and Form 541 information, and photos where available.

It is possible that two aircraft carried the same code on a Squadron, as aircraft came back from modification programmes and older standard aircraft with the same code stayed on charge for a short while.

102 Above: The Queen meets some of the members of the RAF, many of whom had extensive operational experience from World War II, as shown by the many decorations being worn. This picture was taken behind the FTC Ansons, C.19 VM313/34 being visible immediately behind the Queen

103 Left: This was the scene sometime between 12.00 and 12.35 following the parading of the RAF Colour soon after the Queen had inspected the Parade. The men (and women) march past the Royal dais to the accompaniment of the music provided by the six bands of the RAF and WRAF

SERIAL/CODE TIE-UPS

Chipmunk T.10 RAF College
WB601	WK570/DV
WB616	WK573
WB688	WK612/DX
WB689	WP838/JA
WB692	WP844
WB724	WP845/JI or JT
WB755	WP849
WD304	WP853
WG353	WP854
WK517/DA	WP855/DC
WK518/DB	WP856
WK554/DD	WP857/JC
WK555	WP858
WK556/DK	WP859/JP
WK557/DG	WP860
WK558/DH	WP862
WK559/DJ	WP863/JH
WK560	WP864/JJ
WK561/DL	WP865/JK
WK562/DM	WP866
WK563/DN	WP868/JM
WK564	WP869/JN
WK565/DP	WP903
WK566/DR	WP904
WK567/DS	WP905/JR
WK568/DT	WZ865/JV
WK569/DU	WZ875

Balliol T.2 7 FTS
WF989/Q-Q or D-E	WG126/D-U
WF990	WG127/D-V
WF991	WG128/D-W
WF992/Q-D	WG129
WF993/Q-C	WG130
WF995	WG131/D-A
WF996/Q-Y	WG132/D-B
WF997	WG133/D-C
WF998	WG134/D-D
WG110	WG135/D-E
WG111/Q-H	WG136/D-F
WG112/Q-T	WG137
WG114/Q-U	WG138/D-G
WG117/Q-S	WG139/D-H
WG118/Q-X	WG140
WG119/D-O	WG141
WG120/D-Q	WG179/Q-A
WG121/D-R	WG186
WG123/D-S	WG187
WG124/D-T	

Note: Either WF997 or WG141 was Q-E.

Vampire NF.10 23 Squadron
WM670	WP248/B
WM704	WP251
WM705	WP253
WM706	WP254/F
WM730	WP255
WP236	WP256/E

Vampire NF.10 25 Squadron
WM668/E	WP238/M or N
WM672/Q	WP239/P
WM713	WP242/N
WP233/A	WP245/O or J
WP234	WP246/D
WP235/D	WP252/B

Venom FB.1
WE306/B-P   Wing Leader Wunsdorf

Venom FB.1 5 Squadron
WE273	WE329/B-X
WE292/B-Q	WE332
WE310/B-F	WE341/B-A
WE311	WE342/B-M
WE319/B-C	WE344/B-A
WE321/B-L	WE346/B-N
WE323/B-D	WE347/B-E
WE325/B-G	WE350/B-K

Venom FB.1 11 Squadron
WE283/L-H	WE305/L-T
WE284/L-B	WE307/L-W
WE285/L-C or L-L	WE309/L-P
WE286/L-N	WE317/L-S
WE287/L-O	WE340
WE290	WE343
WE291/L-U	WE345/L-A
WE293/L-D	WE352/L-K

Venom FB.1 CFE
WE261	WE275
WE263	WE313
WE264	WE314
WE265	

Note: W/C Bird-Wilson's records show that WE261, WE263, WE275, WE313 and WE314 were the aircraft modified with smoke devices for the review.

Meteor F.8
Station Flight/Wing Leader Aircraft
VZ468	Stn Flt Leuchars
VZ484	Met Sector West Malling
WA764/LHB	Stn Flt/W.L. Wattisham
WA965	Stn Flt Biggin Hill
WA983	Stn Flt Duxford
WF677/RWO	Stn Flt/W.L. Church Fenton
WF695/RDY	Stn Flt Horsham St Faith
WH401/LM	Stn Flt/W.L. Linton
WH415/PB	Stn Flt/W.L. Waterbeach
WH444/CM	Stn Flt/W.L. Odiham
WK689/NW	Stn Flt North Weald
WK724/HH	Northern Sector, Linton
WK731/JAK	Stn Flt Tangmere
WK787/CGL	Caledonian Sector
WK795/JW or SCW	Eastern Sector, Horsham
WK865	W.L. Met. Sector North Weald

Meteor F.8 54 Squadron
WA825	WH471/Z
WE876	WK673/Y
WH345/B	WK707/O
WH370/R	WK709/V
WH378/N	WK710/A
WH396/H	WK712/J
WH397/K	WK879/C
WH404/T	

Meteor F.8 247 Squadron
WE866/V	WK671/Z
WE873/R or D	WK672/X
WF742	WK725/B
WF756/N	WK785/H
WH426/T	WK810
WH443/W	WK825/Q
WH468/S	WK874/C
WK654/E	WK876/F
WK668/A	

Meteor F.8 1 Squadron
VZ458/B	WA855/O
VZ496/J	WA856/C
VZ548/G	WA868/D
VZ549/F	WA872/R
VZ552/W	WF642/T
WA842/A	WH286/S
WA845/E	WK908/L
WA853/Z	WK916/X
WA854/N	WK917/V

Meteor F.8 41 Squadron
WA929/W	WE975/H
WA991/D	WF681/R
WA994/Q,R,V or X	WF702/T
WB111/A	WH368/L or Y
WE853/X	WH480/M or X
WE859/C	WK888/B
WE943/G	WK892/V
WE949/E or F	WK951/S

Meteor F.8 64 Squadron
WA896/A	WH460/B
WE923/G	WH484/Z
WE926/E	WK659/D
WE927/C	WK887
WE952/S	WK966
WF713/U	WK968/F
WH313/J	WK970/W
WH314/H	WK978/P

Meteor F.8 65 Squadron
VZ532/E	WF704/B
WA963/F	WF737/O
WE920/R	WF738/A
WE921/U or W	WH306/C
WE974/N	WH459/Q
WF659/P	WK681/H
WF660/S	WK801/G
WF703/J	WK827/T

Meteor F.8 245 Squadron
VZ559/E	WK882/X
VZ565/Y	WK886/J
WA773/B	WK890/R
WE901/Z	WK891/A
WF679/D	WK893/G
WF712	WK928/C
WF740/K	WK932/M
WH416/F	WK934/T
WK820/N	WK936/H
WK863/S	WK947/W
WK880/Q	WK950/P
WK881/V	

Note: WK890 did not arrive on the Squadron until 14 July 1953.

Meteor F.8 74 Squadron
VZ512/D	WA997/R
VZ521/A	WE885/G
VZ524/P	WE960/U
VZ529/V	WF647/S
VZ544/X	WF651/T
VZ557/N	WF652/Z
WA824/Q	WF656/Y
WA838/F	WF708/H
WA874/K	WH357/M
WA879/C	WK804/B

Meteor F.8 63 Squadron
VZ464/H	WA989/F
VZ568/C	WA993/O
WA765/B	WE852/L
WA768/U	WE884/Y
WA812/N	WE938/K
WA818/V	WF650/W
WA819/M	WF705/J
WA846/S or E	WH374/A
WA897/P	WH377/T
WA903/D	WH449/R
WA923/X	WK658/G

91

Meteor F.8 56 Squadron
VZ480/F	WA999/K
VZ483/T	WE875/L
VZ540/O	WE883/M
WA767/G or U	WE951/V
WA769/G	WF643/J
WA905/W	WF689/B
WA922/D	WF709/Y
WA924/R	WH283/A
WA927/X	WH446/S
WA928/H	WH510/E
WA930/C	WK726/P

Meteor F.8 66 Squadron
VZ440/P	WF655/E or T
VZ567/W	WF680/T
WA778/U	WF715/H
WA785/E	WH508/F
WA850/D	WK718/Q
WE959/L	WK719/C
WE961/N	WK738/M
WE964/B	WK741

Note: WA850 did not arrive on the Squadron until 11 July 1953.

Meteor F.8 92 Squadron
VZ462/B or Y	WE925/E
VZ485/F or W	WE973/R
VZ511/V	WF646
VZ564/S	WF649/Z
WA761/U	WF711/J
WA813/C	WF753/H
WA906/D	WH403/Q
WA921/P	WK799/A

Meteor F.8 257 Squadron
VZ444/B	WA891/E
VZ467/D	WA955/K
VZ471/M	WF648
VZ541/Y or F	WH258
VZ561/X	WH291/V
WA817/H	WH297/A
WA875/T	WH298/Z
WA880/S	WH300/U
WA886/R	WK943/N
WA890/L	

Note: WH258 was with the unit from 14 July until 3 August 1953.

Meteor F.8 263 Squadron
VZ545/A	WE915/J
WA757/G	WE935/K
WA793/U	WF755/B
WA885/H	WH287/S
WA893/C	WH296/W
WA920/P	WH299/L
WA926/Y	WH382/V

WA943/Z	WH467
WA959/M	WH476/E
WA967/R	WK911/F
WA986/Q or T	

Note: WA967 did not arrive on the Squadron until 13 July 1953.

Meteor F.8 43 Squadron
VZ441/T	WA871/E
VZ452/O	WA899/G
VZ513/Y	WA992/D
VZ514/Z	WK814/PM
WA794/X	WK856
WA841/M	WK859
WA844/N	WK871/W
WA847/P	WK873/H
WA849/R	

Meteor F.8 222 Squadron
VZ448/A	WH453
VZ515/F	WH466/R
VZ516/C or H	WK861
VZ523/Q	WK869
VZ554/N	WK918/S
WA814/D	WK921/E
WA869	WK939
WA933/P or O	

Meteor F.8 72 Squadron
VZ525/N	WK679/B
WA831/S	WK691/X
WF743/V	WK714/G
WH304/Y	WK736/P
WH305/O	WK750/C
WH463/F	WK751/D
WH500/H	WK974/E
WK656/A	WK977/T
WK677/R	

Meteor F.8 19 Squadron
WA758/N or X	WE856/G
WA816/M	WE857/P
WA969/E	WE863/A
WB105/O	WE870/G
WB107/K	WH275/H
WB108/F	WH348/Y
WB109/R	WK734/L
WE855/C	WK914/B

Note: WE870 did not arrive on the Squadron until 5 July 1953.

Meteor NF.11
WD780	Stn Flt Coltishall
WM154	Stn Flt West Malling

Meteor NF.11 85 Squadron
WD614/M	WD625/R

WD615/A	WD763/H
WD616/B	WM174
WD618/C	WM175/Y
WD619/D	WM176
WD620/O	WM177

Meteor NF.11 29 Squadron
WD597/B	WD605/D
WD598/T	WD715/W
WD599/P	WD722/E
WD600/S	WD725/F
WD602/A	WD762/X
WD603/C	WD792/U

Meteor NF.11 151 Squadron
WD593/A	WM148/K
WD629/C	WM155/H
WD630/D	WM251/Q
WD640/O	WM260/E
WD738/W	WM267/X
WD787/T	WM270/J

Meteor NF.11 141 Squadron
WD610/T	WM160/R
WD611/U	WM162/X
WD612/V	WM164/Y
WD644/W	WM225/M
WM157/N	WM255/S

Meteor NF.11 264 Squadron
WD647/S	WD660/L
WD649/C	WD661/M
WD650/B	WD665/R
WD652/E	WD710/P or Q
WD655/A	WD724/F
WD657/D	WD783/N

Sabre F.4
XB619 Wing Leader Wildenrath

Sabre F.4 3 Squadron
XB536/Z	XB640/P
XB541/L	XB644/K
XB581/T	XB670/S
XB582	XB672/G
XB590/V	XB681/J
XB609/poss H	XB684/Q
XB612/F	XB703/Y
XB614/B	XB740/M
XB617/C	XB744/A
XB633/N or W	

Note: XB582 became 'R', but was uncoded in the static display.

Sabre F.4 67 Squadron
XB586/X	XB671/E
XB596/F	XB674/G
XB598/R	XB678/L
XB600/W	XB683/V
XB625	XB690/Z
XB626	XB692/D
XB627/C	XB705
XB639/P	XB730/Y
XB664/B	XB737/A

Note: XB705 became 'S', but was uncoded in the static display.

Sabre F.4 Sabre Conversion Flight Wildenrath
XB542	XB675
XB587	XB676
XB591	XB682
XB592	XB688
XB602	XB700
XB611	XB726
XB616	XB728
XB618	XB738
XB673	

104: Man at work. Canberra WD955 took part in the Flypast as a B.2 of 617 Squadron, flown by F/O John Cochrane, later a Concorde test pilot. It is seen here as a T.17A being flown by the author during an air display over Salmesbury in May 1987. It was described by the show commentator as "the oldest Canberra flown by the oldest test pilot"

PARTICIPATING PILOTS

F/L	FA	Abbott
F/O	AEG	Abczynski
S/L	JI	Adams (RAAF)
F/L	DT	Adamson
F/O	JCL	Ainger
S/L	RI	Alexander
W/C	JW	Allan
F/O	BE	Allen
Maj	MF	Allen (USAF)
F/O	C	Allsop
F/O	NG	Allsop
F/O	AK	Amos
S/L	KC	Andrews (RAAF)
F/L	B	Appleyard
Capt	HB	Arnold (USAF)
F/O	BA	Ashley
F/L	RCB	Ashworth
F/L	DH	Atherton (RCAF)
F/O	D	Auty
F/O	RN	Baff
F/L	GM	Bailey
F/L	GD	Bain
F/O	SW	Bainbridge
W/C	T	Balmforth
F/L	GD	Banfield
F/L	F	Barnes
W/C	PPC	Barthropp
F/L	C	Bartlett
W/C	LH	Bartlett
S/L	E	Batchelar
F/O	RH	Bateman
F/L	RM	Batten
Mr	R	Baxter
Mr		Baxter
A P/O	C	Beadle
S/L	B	Beard
Sgt	WB	Beck
F/L	EG	Beedle
S/L	H	Bennett
F/O	GJ	Bennett
F/S	RF	Berners
F/L	CH	Biddie
F/O	RR	Biggar (RCAF)
F/O	DC	Bingham
P/O		Bingham
W/C	HAC	Bird-Wilson
P/O	DB	Birley
F/O	J	Birnie
F/O	IMA	Black
F/O	R	Blackburn
F/L	AL	Blackman
F/L	JSF	Blundell
Capt	J	Bodie (USAF)
F/O	GA	Boord
F/O	PG	Botterill
F/L	NE	Bowen
F/L	R	Bowie
F/L	PN	Boyle
S/L	AD	Boyle
F/L	S	Bradford
F/O	MG	Bradley
F/O	RM	Bradley (RCAF)
F/O	KA	Branch (RCAF)
F/L	JH	Bransgrove
Sgt	DV	Brice
F/L	RC	Bridges
F/L	MJ	Bridges
F/L	SJ	Bromley
	L	Brown
F/L	NF	Brown
F/L	HHJ	Browning
F/O	J	Bruce
G/C	GK	Buckingham
F/L	NCP	Buddin
F/L	WH	Burden

F/L	K	Burge
F/L	AC	Burn
W/C	WJ	Burnett
F/L	NA	Burns (RCAF)
F/L	RGM	Burton
F/L		Burton
F/O	J	Bush
F/O	PHJ	Butler
F/S	AL	Button
S/L	JC	Button
F/O	H	Buxton
F/L	BN	Byrne
F/L	NA	Caillard
F/L	JM	Calvey
F/L	RD	Campbell
F/L	DP	Carey
F/S	E	Carlick
F/O		Carpenter
P/O	R	Carus-Davis
S/L	CM	Cassels
F/L	MH	Castle
F/O	AW	Chambers
F/O	JS	Chambers
S/L	B	Champneys
F/O	R	Chapman
Sgt	JK	Cappell
F/O	DG	Cinnamon (RCAF)
Sgt	JS	Clanchy
F/O	GJB	Claridge
F/O	PJ	Clarke
F/O	LE	Clowes
F/O	J	Cochrane
Sgt	GH	Cole
F/O	P	Collins
F/L	RG	Collins
F/O	J	Cookson
F/O	DA	Cooper
F/O	RF	Cooper
F/O	PE	Cornell
F/O	AHP	Cornish
F/S		Coulbeck
Sgt	D	Coupland
F/L	LR	Court
F/S	AE	Cover
F/L	JB	Cowton
F/L	BRA	Cox
P/O	JSD	Craig
S/L	J	Crampton
F/L	DA	Cree
F/O	TJ	Creswell
F/O	KD	Crisp
S/L	MG	Crotty
W/C	D	Crowley-Milling
F/O	JG	Cruse
Sgt	E	Culpin
F/L	RSM	Dadd
F/O	RJ	Davis
F/L		Davies
F/L	JE	Dawes
F/L		Dawes
F/L	TGD	Dawkins
Sgt	CG	Dawson
F/O	LD	Day
F/O	R	Deely
F/O	D	Delaney
F/O	JL	Denouden (RCAF)
F/L	EA	Devillez
F/L	A	Devine
S/L	JFJ	Dewhurst
P/O	R	Dick
F/L	GG	Dillingham
P/O	R	Dixon
F/O	MFH	Dobson
F/L	GH	Dodd
W/C	FL	Dodd

F/L	RE	Dodds
S/L	FW	Doherty
F/O	B	D'Oliviera
Sgt	AIS	Donald
F/L	WS	Donson
W/C	AP	Dottridge
F/O	KG	Dougan
F/O	DEB	Dowling
S/L	NF	Duke
F/L	RHD	Dulieu
P/O	S	Duncan
F/L	DA	Dunlop
S/L	SC	Dunmore
F/O	M	Earle
F/L	RCH	Easy
G/C	BA	Eaton (RAAF)
F/S	AE	Edwards
F/L	HC	Eggins
F/O	WJ	Elford
F/L	JN	Elliman
F/L	JH	Elliott
F/O	DJ	Elsden
F/O	R	Emberson
F/O	DS	Emsley
F/L	NG	Emslie
S/L	MA	Ensor
F/L	KJ	Evans
S/L	VRL	Evans
F/O	AJ	Everard (RCAF)
F/O	D	Everest
F/L	TP	Fargher
F/L	GG	Farley
F/S	WH	Farnell
W/C	RJ	Falk
P/O	EE	Fell
F/L	AA	Fenn
F/O	TM	Fennel
F/O	WW	Ferguson
F/O	HO	Field
F/O	EL	Fine (RCAF)
S/L	GW	O'N Fisher
F/L	EJG	Flavell
Sgt	KE	Fluck
S/L	FR	Flynn
S/L	DG	Ford
F/L	RW	Ford
F/S	JR	Foster
F/L	GA	Francis
F/O	SF	Fraze
Sgt	WHG	Freeman
F/L	NH	Frost
F/L	PJ	Fry
F/L	J	Gale
S/L	EC	Gartrell (RNZAF)
F/L	A	Gavan
F/O	D	Geddes
F/O	JE	George
F/O	MA	George
Sgt	HW	Gibson
F/L	KVE	Gilbert
S/L	WTH	Gill (RCAF)
F/L	RA	Gillam
F/O	JM	Gisborne
F/L	JP	Gledhill
Sgt	RG	Glynn
F/O	A	Goadby
F/O	MC	Goldsmith
F/O	DM	Goodwin
F/O	HJ	Gourley
F/O	CA	Grabham
P/O	MJC	Grant
F/L	JED	Gray
F/O	JL	Gregg
F/O	HG	Haines
F/L	GA	Hamilton

93

F/O	JL	Hamilton (RCAF
Capt	FF	Hamilton (USAF)
F/O	JS	Hannah (RCAF)
F/O	RJM	Haran (RCAF)
S/L	W	Harbison
F/L	MT	Harding-rolls
F/O	JA	Harrison
F/O	M	Hart
F/O	FH	Hartley
F/O		Harty
F/O	AD	Harvie
F/O	RB	Haverstock(RCAF)
S/L	JD	Hawkins
Sgt	MJ	Hawkins
S/L	HG	Hazelden
P/O	JW	Heard
F/L	JH	Hedger
F/L	WE	Hedley
F/O	F	Hercliffe
F/L	GM	Hermitage
F/O	DE	Herrett
F/O	JGF	Hewitt
S/L	SG	Hewitt
S/L	WJ	Hibbert
F/L	PKV	Hicks
F/L	J	Higginbottom
S/L	JS	Higgins
P/O	WM	Hilditch
S/L	JES	Hill
F/S	RPF	Hill
P/O	WW	Hill
F/O	PB	Hine
F/L	JM	Hocking
F/S	CG	Hodkinson
F/L	DH	Hofford
F/L	CK	Holbrook
F/O		Holden
F/L	CJ	Holmes
S/L	LG	Holmes
Sgt	NE	Hollins
P/O	RE	Holloway
Sgt	AA	Holyoake
P/O	EW	Hopkins
F/O	JA	Horrell
F/L	WC	Horsman(RAAF)
F/L	JV	Horwood
F/L	AI	Hoult
S/L	DR	Howard
F/L	KC	Howard
F/L	DM	Howarth
Sgt	GD	Howarth
F/S	AB	Howes
F/L	SJ	Hubbard
S/L	AP	Huchala (RCAF)
F/L	W	Hughes
S/L	CS	Hunton
P/O	D	Hurley
F/L	LG	Hurrell
F/L	AA	Hutchinson
G/C	NC	Hyde
F/L	HJ	Irving
Sgt	PJ	Izzard
F/L	JA	Jackson
F/L	WH	Jackson
F/O		Jackson
P/O	JA	Jacobs(RAAF)
F/O	WS	Jacques
F/L	FR	James
S/L	RWW	James
F/S	M	Jankiewicz
F/L	JB	Jay
F/L	AF	Jenkins
F/O	ST	Jenkins
Sgt	R	Jerka
F/S	J	Jilek
Sgt	JF	Joachim
F/O	TS	Johnson

F/O	WHC	Johnston (RCAF)
F/O	AN	Jones
F/L	EG	Jones
F/O	JFB	Jones
F/O	RH	Jones (RAAF)
F/L	DCL	Kearns
F/O	DJB	Keats
F/O	KP	Kelleher
S/L	PJ	Kelley
F/O	JG	Kemp
F/L	PJ	Kent
F/O	GJ	Kerr (RCAF)
F/S	KS	Kijak
A P/O	BJ	King
F/O	MG	King
F/O	MJ	King
F/L	JH	Kingsbury
F/S	J	Kmiecik
F/O	RM	Knox-Leet (RCAF)
S/L	AEW	Laband
S/L	EP	Landon
F/O	HR	Lane
F/L	TPD	La Touche
Sgt	IH	Laurie
M		Laval
Capt	KL	Lawrence (USAF)
F/O		Lawrence
F/L	JR	Leask
W/C	MH	Le Bas
Sgt	EIV	Lee
Lt		Legg(RN)
S/L	RE	Le Long
F/O	JP	L'Estrange
F/L	DA	Letham
F/L	MH	Levy
F/L	DA	Lewis
S/L	NED	Lewis
F/O	WO	Lewis
F/O	JL	Lingham
F/L	FW	Lister
Lt Cdr	MJ	Lithgow (RN)
F/L	RG	Lofting
Sgt	JJFM	Logan
F/O	RK	Lord
F/L	JS	Luby
Sgt	AJ	McArthur
F/L	DPF	McCaig
P/O	RS	McCarty
Sgt	BADM	Macdonald
F/L	CS	Macdonald
F/O	WG	McEwen (RCAF)
W/C	R	McFarlane
F/O	DC	McIlraith (RCAF)
W/C	G	McKenzie
F/O	NM	Mackerracher (RCAF)
F/O	RE	Mackie
F/L	AJ	Mackinnon
F/L	L	Mackinnon
F/L	R	Maclachlan
F/O		McLean
F/L	RS	McTavish
F/L	JK	Maddison
F/L	LJA	Maisonpierre
W/C	LA	Malins
F/O	PG	Mallett
F/S	WDE	Martin
F/L	JH	Marvin
P/O	B	Mason
W/C	PGH	Matthews
F/L	RS	May
Sgt	CH	Maynard
F/O	SB	Mead
F/L	J	Mellers
F/L	PC	Mellett
F/O	PW	Mepham (RCAF)
F/L	AD	Mercer
F/L	BPW	Mercer

F/O	DB	Merifield
Sgt	AJM	Merry
F/O	WHE	Michelin
S/L	JS	Millington
F/O	BC	Mills
F/O	DH	Mills
F/L	H	Minnis
F/S	K	Miture
Sgt	W	Mode
F/O	EW	Moore
F/O	RB	Morgan
F/O	VJ	Morgan
S/L	RB	Morison
F/L	R	Morris (RCAF)
F/O	D	Morter
S/L	AJ	Mott
S/L	JCM	Mountford
Lt Col	GW	Mulholland (USAF)
F/L	D	Mullarkey
F/O	AW	Mutch
Sgt	AS	Myers
P/O	LS	Naile
F/O	RW	Napier
Sgt	KS	Neate
F/L	CRG	Neville
S/L	AE	Newitt
F/L	RS	Nichol
F/L	GH	Nichols (RCAF)
F/L	JM	Nicholls
F/L	EL	Nieass
F/O	BJ	Noble
Sgt	E	Noble
F/O	MJS	Norman
P/O	RV	Oborn
F/S	BA	O'callaghan
W/C	EFJ	Odoire
F/L	JA	Ormerod
	Q	Oswell
F/O	W	Otty
F/L	AJ	Oury
S/L	JS	Owen
W/C	RW	Oxspring
F/O	RA	Paquett (RCAF)
F/O	JJ	Parker
F/O	MD	Parry
F/L	RA	Patterson
F/O	AGS	Pattinson
S/L	HG	Pattison
F/O	FR	Pearson
F/O	JB	Peart
F/L	JW	Peckowski
F/L	GD	Perks
Capt	MLW	Peters (USAF)
F/L	RS	Peters
F/L	CJ	Petheram
F/S	A	Piercy
F/O	DM	Piercy
P/O	AE	Pike
Sgt	BD	Platt
F/S	S	Pomfret
F/L	EW	Poole
F/O	RS	Poole (RCAF)
F/L	RSG	Poole
M/P	AV	Potter
F/O	KC	Povey
F/L	G	Powell
F/O	JR	Powell
M/P	J	Pratt
F/L	G	Price
F/O	NRC	Price
F/O	P	Price-Whittle
F/L	J	Primrose
F/L	PNB	Pritchett
F/L	NH	Prowting
F/O	GS	Puddy
F/O	TJ	Pugh
Sgt	EW	Quinney

F/L	J	Radomski
F/O	AL	Rackham
F/S	A	Ramsden
F/L	FN	Ramsey
F/O	AA	Ramus
F/O	L	Reading (RAAF)
F/L	BH	Reece
F/O	MF	Reischman (RCAF)
F/O	JT	Reynolds
F/L	DJ	Rhodes
P/O	DG	Riley
Maj	JN	Robb (SAAF)
F/O	BH	Roberts
S/L	D	Roberts
F/O	KBE	Roberts
F/O	PA	Roberts
F/L	JM	Robertson
F/L	LA	Robertson
S/L	WD	Robertson
F/O	AJ	Robson
F/L	KW	Rogers
F/O	EN	Ronaasen (RCAF)
F/O	G	Rorison
F/S	A	Ross
F/L	AM	Ross
F/O	DH	Ross
Sgt	R	Ross
F/O	HC	Ruecker (RCAF)
F/L	GO	Russell
F/S	V	Ryba
F/O	PH	Salter
S/L	TD	Sanderson
Gc	WAJ	Satchell
F/L	AR	Satow
F/S	CE	Saunders
S/L	DC	Saunders
S/L	M	Scannel
F/L	LR	Scholfield
F/O	BW	Scott
M/P	KF	Scott
F/O	L	Scott
F/O	BW	Seaman
S/L	T	Seaton
F/L	J	Severn
F/O	DJ	Seward
F/L	WK	Sewell
F/L	AT	Shaw
F/O	DF	Shaw
Sgt	JE	Shaw
W/C	JT	Shaw
F/O	AE	Sheehan
F/O		Sheppard
F/O	R	Shilton
F/S	JM	Siekierkowski
F/O	MW	Sills (RCAF)
S/L	AH	Simmonds
F/O	EL	Simmonds
F/L	EN	Simmons
F/O	RO	Simmons
F/O	CA	Simpson
S/L	WC	Sinclair
Maj	FE	Singleton(USAF)
S/L	EB	Sismore
F/O	D	Skidmore
F/O	RJ	Skinner
F/O	C	Sly (RAAF)
F/O	DAB	Smiley (RCAF)
F/O	BA	Smith
Sgt	GG	Smith
F/O	GRG	Smith
F/L	JE	Smith
F/S	RB	Smith
F/O	RW	Smith
F/O	TWA	Smith
F/L	WEA	Snelling
F/L	KP	Souter
F/S	JE	Sowerby

F/L	DP	Spencer
F/L	RJ	Spiers
F/O	C	Spooner
S/L	RJS	Spooner
F/O	JC	Sprent
F/L	JH	Spurgeon
F/O	RW	Stafford
F/O	PT	Staton
S/L	CM	Stavert
F/L	AG	Steele
F/L	JA	Stephen
F/O	JB	Stephens
S/L	E	Stephenson
W/C	CLW	Stewart
F/L	EM	Stewart
F/L		Stewart
F/L	EE	Stocker
F/L	GB	Stockman
F/O	PD	Stonham
F/O	PAL	Stott
S/L	G	Strange
F/L	JGW	Stroud
Sgt	JG	Stuart
F/L	RH	Stubbs
F/O	K	Sturt
S/L	WJS	Sutherland
F/O	J	Sutton
P/O	IAG	Svensson
F/L	DW	Swart
F/S	W	Szmaciarz
M/P	W	Sznapka
F/L	WR	Tait
F/O	DV	Tann
F/L	DW	Tanner
F/L	JR	Tanner
F/L	AR	Taylor
S/L	EH	Taylor
F/L	CJ	Tedder
F/O	A	Temperton
F/L	FA	Thomas
M/P	OJ	Thomas
F/L	P	Thomas
F/O	R	Thomas
F/L	CFP	Thompson
F/O	WH	Thompson (RCAF)
F/L	G	Thornton (RAAF)
F/L	G	Thrower
F/O	PJ	Thrower
F/S	J	Tichy
F/S	NE	Tindal
F/L	EB	Trubshaw
S/L	HMH	Tudor
F/O	D	Turgoose
F/L	AH	Turner
S/L	GR	Turner
F/L	JC	Turner (RCAF)
Sgt	RL	Turner
F/O	AR	Twigger
A/C	SR	Ubee
S/L	DC	Usher
F/L	F	Val-Jones
F/L	N	Varanand
Sgt	RL	Vickers
F/L	J	Villeneuve (RCAF)
F/O	HMcC	Vincent
F/S	VAL	Volanthen
F/O	C	Walker
F/L	S	Walker
W/C	J	Wallace
F/L	DE	Walton
F/O	PR	Ward
F/O	AR	Wardell
F/L	MH	Ware
F/L	RJE	Wareham
F/L	TA	Warren
Sgt	MW	Warrick
S/L	WA	Waterton

F/L	DJ	Watkins
F/O	PR	Watson
F/O	R	Watson
F/O		Watson
Sgt	H	Watt
F/L	WN	Waudby
F/O	WR	Webster
F/S	JC	Wellby
Sgt	D	Wells
F/L	HF	Wenz (RCAF)
S/L	CS	West
P/O	LB	Weymouth (RAAF)
F/L	DS	White
W/C	HNG	Wheeler
F/L	PJ	Whittaker
F/L	ME	Whitworth-Jones
F/L	WK	Wightman
F/O	PJ	Wilde
F/S	RG	Wilding
F/O	GE	Williams
F/L	JA	Williams
F/O	CK	Williamson
F/O	DR	Williamson (RCAF)
F/O	KM	Williamson
F/L	AGS	Wilson
F/O	PF	Wilson
S/L	RG	Wilson
S/L	RK	Wilson
Sgt	JF	Winchester
F/O	HRR	Wingate (RCAF)
F/O	KAC	Wirdnam
M/P	A	Wiseman
F/O	DJ	Wistow
F/O	S	Wood
F/O	BW	Woodfield
F/L	VD	Woods
F/O		Woollard
F/L	MJ	Woodyer
F/L	IAN	Worby
F/L	JA	Worrall
F/L	BE	Wrensch
F/O	A	Wright
F/O	AWA	Wright
S/L	FCD	Wright
F/O	GE	Wright
F/L	KB	Wright
Sgt	N	Wright
F/L	JG	Wynne
S/L	DA	Young
Sgt	M	Young
F/O	RI	Young
W/C	RD	Yule
F/S	K	Zmitrowicz
F/S	Z	Zmitrowicz

Sgt	Sergeant
F/S	Flight Sergeant
P/O	Pilot Officer
F/O	Flying Officer
F/L	Flight Lieutenant
S/L	Squadron Leader
W/C	Wing Commander
G/C	Group Captain
A/C	Air Commodore
M/P	Master Pilot
Capt	Captain
Maj	Major
Lt Col	Lieutenant Colonel

CAPTIONS TO COLOUR ILLUSTRATIONS

Inside front cover
1 Gloster Meteor F.8, WH359/K of 611 Sqn. Inset: 611 Sqn. badge.
2 Gloster Meteor F.8, WK799/A of 92 Sqn.
3 Gloster Meteor F.8, WK738/M of 66 Sqn.
4 Gloster Meteor F.8, WK722/A of 601 Sqn. Inset: 601 Sqn badge
5 Gloster Meteor F.8, WK784, the C.O's aircraft of 604 Sqn.
6 Gloster Meteor F.8, WH480 of 41 Sqn.

Page 49
7 Supermarine Spitfire 16, TE389/C of a A.A.C.U.
8 N.A. Harvard T.2B, KF165/E-O of 6 F.T.S. Inset: 6 F.T.S badge
9 N.A. Harvard T.2B, KF280/N-Q of 1 F.T.S.
10 Taylorcraft Auster AOP.6, VF607/J of 664 Sqn.
11 Avro Anson C.19, VL312/25 of 527 Sqn. Inset: 527 Sqn. badge.
12 Avro Anson C.19, VM313/34 of 116 Sqn. Inset: 116 Sqn. badge.

Page 50
13 De Havilland Devon C.1, VP966, of FTCCS.
14 Percival Prentice T.1, VS689/M-L, of 2 FTS.
15 De Havilland Vampire F.B.5, VZ128/0-52 OF of 206 A.F.S.
16 De Havilland Vampire F.B.5, VZ271/Q3-H of 613 Sqn. Inset: 613 Sqn. Badge.
17 De Havilland Vampire F.B.5, VZ812/LO-C of 602 Sqn.
18 De Havilland Vampire F.B.5, WA294/V9-C of 502 Sqn. Inset: 502 Sqn. badge.

Page 51
19 Boeing Washington B.1, WF572/N of 35 Sqn. Inset: 35 Sqn. badge.
20 Handley Page Victor prototype, WB771.
21 Vickers Valiant, 2nd prototype, WB215.
22 Avro Vulcan prototype, VX770.
23 Short Sunderland MR.5, ML763, B-R of 230 Sqn.

Page 52
24 Canadair Sabre 2, 19176, AM-176 of 410 Sqn. RCAF.
25 Canadair Sabre 2, 19188, 88 of 439 Sqn. RCAF. Inset: 439 fin marking.
26 Canadair Sabre F.4, XB626 of 67 Sqn., 2 TAF, Germany.
27 Canadair Sabre F.4, XB640/P of 3 Sqn., 2 TAF, Germany.
28 Hawker Hunter F.1, WT555, first production aircraft.
29 Gloster Javelin, 3rd Prototype. WT827.

Page 53
30 Gloster Meteor F.3, EE359, from 33 M.U.
31 Gloster Meteor F.8, VZ554/ZD-N of 222 Sqn. Note: Codes still in use on this date. Inset: 222 Sqn. badge.
32 Gloster Meteor F.8, VZ557/N of 74 Sqn. Inset: 74 Sqn. badge.
33 Gloster Meteor F.8, WA794/X of 43 Sqn.
34 Gloster Meteor T.7, WL361/X-71 of 203 A.F.S.
35 Gloster Meteor T.7, WA661/M-58 of 206 A.F.S.

Page 54
36 Avro Lincoln B.2, SX926 of 61 Sqn.
37 Avro Lincoln B.2, RA665 of 57 Sqn. Inset: 57 Sqn. badge.
38 Avro Lincoln B.2, RE309/D of Central Navigation & Control School, RAF Shawbury. Details of badge on nose unknown.
39 Avro Lincoln B.2, RE311/48 of 116 Sqn. Inset: 116 Sqn. badge.
40 Avro Lincoln B.2, RE411 of 100 Sqn.
41 Avro Lincoln B.2, RF448 of 230 O.C.U.

Page 55
42 Bristol Freighter Mk.31, NZ5909, of 41 Sqn. RNZAF.
43 Handley Page Hastings C.1, TG560, 'IRIS II' of the Central Signals Establishment, Signals Command.
44 Handley Page Hastings MET.1, TG622/A-C of 202 Sqn.
45 Handley Page Hastings C.(VIP) 4, WD500, of 24 Sqn. Part of the static display. Inset: Transport Command badge.
46 Handley Page Hastings C.2, WJ327, of the RAF Flying College. Inset: RAFFC badge.

Page 56
47 Handley Page Hastings C.2, WJ337/GAF, of 511 (or 99) Sqn. RAF Transport Command. RAFTC badge aft of cockpit.
48 Avro Shackleton MR.1, WB819/B of 269 Sqn.
49 Avro Shackleton MR.2, WL737, T-K of 220 Sqn.
50 Supermarine Swift F.1, WK195.
51 Supermarine Swift F.4, WK198. Piloted by Mike Lithgow, captured World Speed record at 735.7 mph, Tripoli, Libya, on Sept. 26, 1953.
52 Bristol Sycamore HC.12, WV783/F-X of Anti-Submarine Warfare Development Unit.

Page 57
53 Avro Lancaster GR.3, RE164/H-U of Maritime Reconnaissance School. Inset: School of Maritime Reconnaissance badge.
54 Vickers Valetta C.2, VX576 of 30 Sqn. RAFTC badge under cockpit.
55 Vickers Valetta T.3, WJ461/A of 1 Air Navigation School. Inset: 1 A.N.S. badge.
56 Vickers Varsity T.1, WF429/K of 2 A.N.S. Inset: 2 A.N.S.. badge.
57 Lockheed Neptune MR.1, WX521/B-L of 203 Sqn. Inset: 203 Sqn. badge.

Page 58
58 De Havilland Vampire F.B.9, WX213 from 19 M.U.
59 De Havilland Vampire F.B.5, WE836/B of 614 Sqn.
60 De Havilland Vampire FB.5, WA194/18-N of 202 AFS.
61 De Havilland Vampire NF.10, WP233/A of 25 Sqn. Inset: 25 Sqn. badge.
62 De Havilland Vampire NF.10, WP256 of 23 Sqn. Inset: 23 Sqn. badge.
63 De Havilland Vampire T.11, WZ566/31 of 208 A.F.S.

Page 59
64 De Havilland Vampire T.11, WZ570/N-50 of 202 A.F.S.
65 De Havilland Vampire T.11, WZ561/0-55 of 206 A.F.S.
66 De Havilland Venom FB.1, WE319/B-C of 5 Sqn. Inset: 5 Sqn. badge.
67 De Havilland Venom FB.1, WE264 of C.F.E.
68 De Havilland Venom FB.1, WE345/L-A of 11 Sqn. Inset: 11 Sqn. badge.
69 De Havilland Venom F.B.1, WE326/A-A of 266 Sqn. Tip tank markings are provisional and reflect the tonal values evident in the reference photograph on page 20.

Page 60
70 Gloster Meteor F.8, WA845/E of 1 Sqn.
71 Gloster Meteor F.8, WE863/A of 19 Sqn.
72 Gloster Meteor F.8, WH397/K of 54 Sqn. Inset: 54 Sqn. badge.
73 Gloster Meteor F.8, WK726/P of 56 Sqn.
74 Gloster Meteor F.8, WK658/G of 63 Sqn.
75 Gloster Meteor F.8, WE927/C of 64 Sqn.

Page 61
76 Gloster Meteor F.8, WK681/H of 65 Sqn.
77 Gloster Meteor F.8, WK679/B of 72 Sqn.
78 Gloster Meteor F.8, WE901/Z of 245 Sqn.
79 Gloster Meteor F.8, WK672/X of 247 Sqn.
80 Gloster Meteor F.8, WK943/N of 257 Sqn.
81 Gloster Meteor F.8, WA893/C of 263 Sqn. Inset: 263 Sqn. nacelle marking.

Page 62
82 Gloster Meteor F.8, WH451/G of 500 Sqn.
83 Gloster Meteor F.8, WA465/Y of 600 Sqn.
84 Gloster Meteor F.8, WH293/B of 610 Sqn. Inset: 610 Sqn. badge.
85 Gloster Meteor F.8, WK754/WH-S of A.P.S.
86 Gloster Meteor T.7, WG946/Y-72 of 206 A.F.S.
87 Gloster Meteor T.7, WH194/S-19 of 207 A.F.S.

Page 63
88 Gloster Meteor F.8, WK692/F of 604 Sqn.
89 Gloster Meteor NF.11, WD603/C of 29 Sqn.
90 Gloster Meteor NF.11, WD763/H, the C.O's aircraft of 85 Sqn.
91 Gloster Meteor NF.11, WD618/C of 85 Sqn.
92 Gloster Meteor NF.11, WM260/E of 151 Sqn.
93 Gloster Meteor NF.11, WM164/Y of 141 Sqn. Inset: 141 Sqn. badge.

Page 64
94 Gloster Meteor F.8, WH444 of RAF Odiham Station Flight.
95 Gloster Meteor F.8, WH401/ L-M. The code is the initials of W/C L.G. Martin, of RAF Linton-on-Ouse.
96 Gloster Meteor F.8, WA764 of RAF Wattisham Station Flight. 263 Sqn. markings carried on port nose with 257 Sqn. markings on the starboard. Inset: 257 and 263 Sqns markings.
97 E.E. Canberra B.2, WH856 of 10 Sqn. Inset: Sqn. nose and tip tank markings.
98 E.E. Canberra B.2, WH640 of 109 Sqn. Inset: 109 Sqn. badge.
99 E.E. Canberra PR.3, WE144 of 540 Sqn.

Inside rear cover
100 Boulton Paul Balliol T.2, WG131/D-A of 7 F.T.S.
101 Percival Provost T.1, WV427 of Central Flying School. Inset: C.F.S. badge.
102 Kirby Cadet KX.3, XA302 of the Air Training Corps.
103 DHC Chipmunk T.10, WZ865/JV of R.A.F. College. Inset: R.A.F.C. badge.
104 Airspeed Oxford T.2, X6781/S-P of 8 F.T.S.
105 Airspeed Oxford T.2, DF418/M-X of 10 AFTS.

Outside rear cover
Captions for colour drawings 106-111 can be found on page 2.